THE SINKING OF THE
BISMARCK

THE DEADLY HUNT

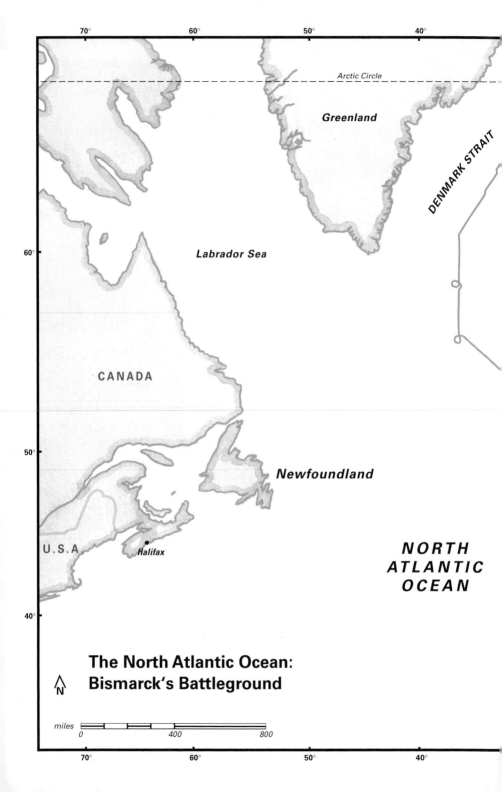

The *Bismarck*

THE SINKING OF
THE *BISMARCK*

THE DEADLY HUNT

WILLIAM SHIRER

ILLUSTRATED WITH PHOTOGRAPHS & MAPS

STERLING

New York / London
www.sterlingpublishing.com/kids

STERLING and the distinctive Sterling logo are registered trademarks of
Sterling Publishing Co., Inc.

A FLYING POINT PRESS BOOK

Design: PlutoMedia
Front cover painting: Grzegorz Nawrocki
Back cover and frontispiece photographs: John Asmussen
(www.bismarck-class.dk)
Interior photographs: John Asmussen and Michael Pocock
(www.maritimequest.com)

Library of Congress Cataloging-in-Publication Data Available

Lot#:
6 8 10 9 7 5
02/11

Published by Sterling Publishing Co., Inc.
387 Park Avenue South, New York, NY 10016
Original edition published by Random House, Inc.
Copyright © 1962 by William L. Shirer
New material in this updated edition
Copyright © 2006 by Flying Point Press
Maps copyright © by Sophie Kittredge, Creative Freelancers, Inc.
Distributed in Canada by Sterling Publishing
c/o Canadian Manda Group, 165 Dufferin Street
Toronto, Ontario, Canada M6K 3H6
Distributed in the United Kingdom by GMC Distribution Services
Castle Place, 166 High Street, Lewes, East Sussex, England BN7 1XU
Distributed in Australia by Capricorn Link (Australia) Pty. Ltd.
P.O. Box 704, Windsor, NSW 2756, Australia

Printed in China
All rights reserved

Sterling ISBN 978-1-4027-3616-2

For information about custom editions, special sales, premium and
corporate purchases, please contact Sterling Special Sales
Department at 800-805-5489 or specialsales@sterlingpublishing.com.

CONTENTS

MAPS

THE SINKING OF THE
BISMARCK

THE DEADLY HUNT

CHAPTER 1

THE MIGHTY *BISMARCK* GOES TO SEA

IT WAS A DARK AND PERILOUS TIME FOR GREAT BRITAIN.

The second spring of World War II had come, and the British stood alone against the seemingly invincible might of the German armed forces.

Germany, which had provoked the war on September 1, 1939, by attacking Poland, had conquered most of Europe. In 1940, led by the ruthless Nazi dictator, Adolf Hitler, the Germans had overrun Norway and Denmark, Holland, Belgium and France. And they had chased the remains of the British Expeditionary Force across the English Channel. After the fall of France, in late June, 1940, Italy had come into the war on the side of Germany. Under another fascist dictator, Benito Mussolini, Italy was threatening the British position in the Mediterranean Sea and in Egypt.

At the beginning of April, 1941, the victorious German army had advanced into Yugoslavia and Greece in the Balkans and quickly occupied them. The British, who had come to the aid of the gallant but small Greek forces, were pushed out of the mainland of Greece. They were trying to make a stand on the Greek island of Crete.

At home, England was taking a severe battering from German bombers. All that winter of 1940–41 the Nazi planes had come over night and day, dropping their lethal loads. Large areas of London and other cities lay in ruins.

At sea, the British, whose navy had ruled the waves for centuries, were in a desperate situation. And it was getting worse.

Since their summer conquests of 1940, the Germans had been able to utilize the harbors and airfields along the coast of western Europe. These stretched from northern Norway to southern France. From their new bases German submarines, warships and bombers had ranged out to sea and taken a fearful toll of British shipping, on which the very existence of Britain depended. By the spring of 1941, British shipping losses had become so great that there was a grave question whether the island nation could hold out.

In February and March of that year, the powerful new German battle cruisers, *Scharnhorst* and *Gneisenau*, broke out into the Atlantic and sank twenty-two British merchant ships. They then managed to get back to the French port of Brest.

Early in May the British Admiralty learned that the new German battleship *Bismarck*, the most powerful warship afloat in the world, had completed her trials in the Baltic. Any day now she might put out to sea to prey on British shipping.

Many of Britain's battleships and aircraft carriers were not available for use against the *Bismarck* in the Atlantic. They were on duty in the Mediterranean trying to check Italy, which had a large navy of her own. They were also busy helping the British armies fighting the Germans in Greece and the Italians in North Africa.

On the morning of May 20, 1941, the Germans launched the greatest airborne attack in the annals of warfare on the British positions in Crete. A large part of the British

Mediterranean fleet rushed to the scene to help the army, which faced another defeat. There was gloom in London as news of the German airborne onslaught came in. But deeper gloom was to come from other news the next day.

At 8:00 A.M. on May 21, a coded message arrived at the Admiralty in London from a British agent in Sweden. On the previous afternoon he had seen from the Swedish shore two large German warships steaming north through the strait between Sweden and Denmark. The ships were obviously en route to German-held Norway, from whose many harbors and fjords German warships in recent months had broken out into the Atlantic.

Admiral Sir John Tovey

The ominous report was flashed at once to Sir John Tovey, commander in chief of the Home Fleet. He was on his flagship, *King George V*, at Scapa Flow, the great naval base in the Orkney Islands at the northern tip of the British Isles. Sir John was a wiry little man of quiet temperament, who remained calm in emergencies. He had a reputation in the navy for spreading confidence, and even optimism, among his officers and his men.

The news he received on the morning of May 21 did not surprise or shake him. But he realized its importance. He immediately summoned his staff officers to discuss it. Their task was to ascertain which German warships were putting to sea, what they were up to, and where. Then they could take appropriate counteraction.

Admiral Tovey was quite sure that the reported German warships were the battleship *Bismarck* and a heavy cruiser of the *Hipper* class. From naval intelligence he knew their fighting qualities.

I myself had seen the *Bismarck* and the cruiser *Admiral Hipper* in the naval yard at Hamburg on Christmas Day the year before. There I had had an opportunity to learn something about these ships. In their respective classes, they were more powerful than any British or American ships then afloat. I knew that the German government had lied in officially listing their size.

At this time the British and American navies were still abiding by a disarmament treaty which limited battleships to 35,000 tons and heavy cruisers to 10,000 tons, but the Germans, while listing their warships at approximately those figures, were actually building them bigger. The *Bismarck* displaced 42,800 tons; the *Hipper*-class cruisers, 14,000 tons. (The German battle cruisers *Scharnhorst* and *Gneisenau*, though registered as 28,000-ton ships, were in reality 31,300-ton vessels.)

The *Bismarck* was easily the most powerful battleship afloat. It had eight 15-inch guns in four turrets, two fore and two aft. It had eighty-one smaller guns, mostly anti-aircraft. It had a speed of twenty-eight knots which could be increased to thirty-one knots at extreme pressure. The most heavily armored ship yet built, it had the additional protection of a special anti-torpedo belt of nickel-chrome-steel. No torpedo then in use by the British—or so the Germans believed—could penetrate this belt. The Germans were convinced that the *Bismarck* was practically unsinkable. And so it turned out to be, as we shall see.

What the German battleship was up to, Admiral Tovey

could easily guess. It would be gunning for British shipping in the Atlantic. At that moment ten precious convoys were at sea. An eleventh convoy was scheduled to sail the next day for the Middle East. This was the most precious of all. It had 20,000 British troops aboard. Not one of these convoys had sufficient naval protection to stand up to the mighty *Bismarck*.

What did the British navy have in fighting ships to match the *Bismarck*? And, more important to Sir John, what did they have to catch and sink her?

No single capital ship in the British fleet could match the *Bismarck* with the possible exception of the 42,000-ton battle cruiser *Hood*, the largest vessel in the British navy and its great pride. But the *Hood*, like all battle cruisers, had sacrificed armor protection for speed.

Admiral Tovey knew that he was superior in numbers. He had in his Home Fleet at Scapa Flow two new 35,000-ton battleships, *King George V*, his flagship, and her sister ship, *Prince of Wales*. He also had the *Hood*. A brand-new aircraft carrier, *Victorious*, was at Scapa taking on planes. But she was due to sail the next day with the battle cruiser *Repulse* to escort the convoy of 20,000 troops for Egypt. Did he dare detach these two big ships from the convoy and risk losing 20,000 soldiers at sea? It was an agonizing question. But there were others.

First, was it really the *Bismarck* that a British spy in Sweden had seen putting out to sea? And second, where was she now, twenty-four hours after being sighted off the Swedish shore? He had to find answers to these questions at once.

Two Spitfire reconnaissance planes were sent out shortly before noon on May 21 to comb the Norwegian ports and fjords. One of them sighted two German warships in Grimstad Fjord just south of Bergen and dived in to take photographs.

The pilot thought the ships were cruisers. But when his photographs were developed and scanned by expert naval eyes back in Britain, they revealed that one of the ships was undoubtedly the *Bismarck*. The other was a heavy cruiser of the *Hipper* class, though which one the British did not know.

So the mighty *Bismarck* was found!

At once orders were given to the Coastal Command to send over bombers that night to try to hit the German battleship while she lay at anchor. In the first daylight of the morrow, other planes would attack with torpedoes.

Aerial photograph taken by a reconnaissance plane
of the *Bismarck* at anchor in a Norwegian fjord

Then the weather, which was to play a commanding
role in the ensuing drama, intervened. It grew worse and
worse. Low clouds and fog brought the visibility down
nearly to zero. The British sent out their bombers, but they
could not find the target. Perhaps it was no longer there.
Perhaps the *Bismarck* and her cruiser escort had already
put out for the Atlantic.

On the chance that they might have, Admiral Tovey
moved that night to intercept them. At midnight he dispatched a battle squadron from Scapa Flow under Vice-
Admiral Lancelot Holland. This consisted of Holland's
flagship, the *Hood*, the brand-new battleship *Prince of*

Wales, and six destroyers. The *Prince of Wales* was in fact so new that several parties of civilian mechanics were still working on her. They put out to sea with the ship, continuing their labors, especially on the big 14-inch gun turrets. These were not working very well. The squadron steered a course for Iceland, where it was to cover the Atlantic exits north and south of the island.

There were, in fact, four passages through which the Germans might break out into the North Atlantic. One was the Fair Island channel, sixty miles wide, between the Shetland and Orkney islands. North of this was a wider channel of 150 miles between the Shetlands and the Faroes Islands. Still farther north was the 240-mile-wide channel between the Faroes and Iceland. And between Iceland and Greenland was the Denmark Strait.

The Germans had previously always used the Denmark Strait. Its low clouds and frequent snowstorms provided good cover. And it was farthest from the British naval and air bases. But it had one disadvantage. Though the Strait was some 200 miles wide, an ice pack stretched out from the coast of Greenland toward Iceland. The ice pack narrowed the passage to about sixty miles of navigable water at this time of year. And at the Strait's northeastern end, the British had sown a mine field stretching out for about fifty miles from Iceland's northwest coast.

Admiral Tovey believed the *Bismarck* would probably head for the Denmark Strait. But he could not be sure. He had to guard the other three channels as well. As the morning of May 22 dawned, he did not even know whether the *Bismarck* was still at Bergen or not. Because of the weather, British reconnaissance planes could not find out.

As the day passed, Tovey's anxieties grew. By afternoon, twenty-four hours had gone by since the German battleship was last spotted in Grimstad Fjord. By this time, for all Sir John knew, the enemy might be approaching the Denmark Strait or slipping through one of the more southerly passages, hidden from sight in the bad weather.

Or the *Bismarck* might still be at Bergen. In this case the British warships already searching for her around Iceland would be wasting their fuel. The problem of conserving fuel oil, as we shall see, was to be a vital one for both sides.

Finally, at 4:30 P.M., with the Coastal Command planes of the Royal Air Force still grounded by bad weather, the navy got off one of its own aircraft in a desperate search for the *Bismarck*. This was an American Maryland bomber which had been used by the fleet for target towing. It had no proper navigation instruments or facilities for taking photographs. Nevertheless it made its way through the clouds to the Norwegian coast, and at twilight swept down through an opening over Grimstad Fjord.

The German ships were no longer there! Just to make sure, the plane flew low over the nearby port of Bergen through a hail of German anti-aircraft fire. It found no trace of the *Bismarck* and her cruiser there either. Fearing that he might be shot down any moment, the pilot got off an urgent radio message to Scapa:

"Battleship and cruiser have left!"

On receipt of this message Admiral Tovey lost no time. His Home Fleet weighed anchor at Scapa at ten o'clock that night—as soon as the ships could get up steam. Tovey's flagship, the *King George V*, sailed out in the van, followed by the aircraft carrier *Victorious*. This also was a new ship whose planes had been taken on only the day before. None of her pilots had in fact ever landed on a carrier deck before. They had intended to practice while escorting the convoy of troops to Egypt.

During the night Admiral Tovey's squadron picked up the battle cruiser *Repulse*, which had also been detached from the convoy. The commander in chief sent out new orders to the *Hood*'s squadron, already approaching Iceland. He also radioed the cruisers *Suffolk* and *Norfolk*, under the command of Rear Admiral W. F. Wake-Walker, to increase their vigil in the icy Denmark Strait, where they were already on patrol.

A powerful British armada was now at sea. The search for the *Bismarck* had begun!

CHAPTER 2

THE SHADOWING OF
THE *BISMARCK*

THE GERMANS HAD A SECRET CODE EXPRESSION for the mission of the *Bismarck*. They called it the "Rhine Exercise," after the river Rhine.

The confidential German naval records, captured at the end of the war, reveal the *Bismarck*'s sailing orders. She was to destroy British merchant shipping in the Atlantic and to avoid, if possible, engagements with a strong enemy fleet. But if cornered by British battleships, the *Bismarck* was to fight with all she had.

The German naval command did not believe the *Bismarck* would be caught. She was too fast for the British battleships. There was some danger, of course, that the big warship might be observed breaking out into the Atlantic north or south of Iceland. But the chances of that, it was believed in Berlin, were slim. The top command of the German navy was convinced that the British warships did not yet have radar as the *Bismarck* had.

This was a costly mistake. Radar enables a ship or plane to see through fog or clouds. It bounces an electric impulse against a distant object and retrieves it. A screen reveals the location of the object, its distance, speed and direction. Some of the British warships hunting for the *Bismarck* had radar too, and it was to play a key role in what now ensued.

The mighty *Bismarck*, as we know from the secret German records, sailed from the Baltic port of Gdynia on the evening of May 18, 1941. She was accompanied by the new heavy cruiser (14,000 tons, 8-inch guns) *Prinz Eugen*. They were supposed to have sailed a month earlier. This would have given them the advantage of having dark nights in which to slip past Iceland into the North Atlantic. But the *Prinz Eugen* had hit a British magnetic mine in the Baltic, and been slightly damaged. The repairs had delayed the venture by nearly a month. Now in the arctic waters, close to the midnight sun, there would be no completely dark nights. The delay was to prove costly.

Still, Admiral Guenther Luetjens on his flagship *Bismarck* was confident as he put out to sea. He was a hard-bitten, stern, somewhat sour naval officer. The crews nicknamed him the "Black Devil." He had already enjoyed dizzy success. It was he who had commanded the battle cruisers *Scharnhorst* and *Gneisenau* a few months earlier when they had sunk twenty-two British merchant ships. With the more powerful *Bismarck*, Luetjens was confident that he would be even more successful.

Two German supply ships and five tankers had put out to sea many days before. If Admiral Luetjens needed to refuel at sea or replenish his ammunition stocks, he could depend on them. All of them had slipped through the British and were now at a secret rendezvous in the mid-Atlantic. Four submarines were also gathering there to aid him if necessary.

The German admiral put into Grimstad Fjord just south of Bergen, Norway, at 9:00 A.M. on May 21. He refueled his two ships. There, taking advantage of the low cloud cover, he put out to sea at eleven o'clock that evening. He did not know that a speedy enemy Spitfire

Admiral Guenther Luetjens

reconnaissance plan had spotted and photographed his ship shortly after noon. The plane had not been seen by the ships' lookouts.

But that night, as his squadron sailed north for the Iceland passage, he was informed by Berlin that the British had discovered his leaving the Baltic. The German naval command did not believe the British knew more than that. German reconnaissance planes flew over Scapa Flow on the afternoon of May 22 and reported that the British Home Fleet had not budged from its base. This was good news to the German admiral aboard the *Bismarck*. It meant that the enemy's Home Fleet could not catch up with him now.

Unfortunately for Admiral Luetjens, the report was not accurate. As we know, one squadron of the Home Fleet, including the *Hood* and the *Prince of Wales*, had sailed from Scapa Flow the night of May 21. Through the stormy arctic waters around Iceland it was converging on the German ships. Neither Vice-Admiral Holland aboard the *Hood* nor Admiral Luetjens on the *Bismarck* knew this. Each had no idea where the other was. But they were soon to learn.

THE SHADOWING OF THE *BISMARCK*

Where is the *Bismarck*? That was the question uppermost in the minds of the British naval commanders at sea as the day of May 23 dawned. No trace of her had yet been found.

Normally, scouting planes ranging over the passage routes would have been able to pick her up by now. But low clouds and fog and—in the Denmark Strait—snowstorms had greatly curtailed their work. Most planes had not even been able to take off.

All day long Admiral Tovey on his flagship *King George V*, plowing northwest toward Iceland, waited impatiently for news of the sighting of the *Bismarck*. None came. Toward evening he calculated that the German ships might well have slipped through the Iceland-Faroes channel. It was 240 miles wide and he did not have enough ships to cover it all in the bad weather. As evening came on May 23, Tovey's spirits were none too high. No news about the *Bismarck* was to him bad news.

Shortly before 7:00 P.M., the British heavy cruiser *Suffolk*, on patrol in the Denmark Strait, reached the top of the mine field off the northwest coast of Iceland and turned around. She had been ordered the day before to look for the *Bismarck* entering the Strait between the mine field and the ice pack that stretched out to sea for a hundred miles from Greenland toward Iceland.

The customary savage weather of these northern waters—gales, snowstorms, heavy mist and bitter cold—somewhat subsided toward evening. There was actually clear weather over the ice and for some three miles off it. But to the southeast, toward Iceland, mist and fog still enshrouded the sea.

When Captain R. M. Ellis, commander of the *Suffolk*, turned about, he deliberately steered over from the ice to the edge of the mist. He did not want to be caught in the open by the big guns of the *Bismarck*, should she suddenly appear from the northeast. It would be more difficult to see her from the stern of his ship on the southwest leg of his patrol. Therefore he kept the *Suffolk* close to the edge of the mist so that at any moment she could dive quickly into it and out of sight. In the fog bank he could still get a fix on the enemy ship if she should approach. For un-known to the Germans, Captain Ellis had the latest mod-el radar installed on his cruiser. He had made a study of its use. This study was now to prove its worth.

Fifteen miles south of the *Suffolk*, deep in the mist, was a second heavy cruiser, the *Norfolk*, under the command of Captain A. J. L. Phillips. Also aboard the ship was Rear Admiral Wake-Walker, who commanded the two cruisers on patrol.

The radar on the *Norfolk* was of primitive make and not of

much use in the search. Admiral Wake-Walker had therefore ordered the ship to keep fifteen miles south of the *Suffolk* and well under cover of the mist and fog. To the *Suffolk*, with her new radar gear, he assigned the main job of finding the *Bismarck* should she try to slip through the Denmark Strait.

Having turned about, the *Suffolk* was edging southwest just clear of the line of mist when at 7:22 P.M. a lookout on the starboard aft cried out: "Ship bearing Green 140 [degrees]!" A moment later came a second cry: "Two ships on the same bearing!"

Captain Ellis raced to the starboard side of the bridge. Through his binoculars he saw the outline of the *Bismarck*, followed by a heavy cruiser. She was only 14,000 yards away. Even at 40,000 yards, he knew, the *Bismarck's* 15-inch guns could blow his ship to bits in an instant.

He immediately gave the order: "Hard a-port!" The *Suffolk* turned sharply toward the mist. But a couple of minutes passed before she reached cover. Each second seemed an eternity to the crew. Finally the British cruiser disappeared into the protective fog. Apparently the lookouts on the *Bismarck* had seen nothing.

Captain Ellis was in a happy but ticklish position. He had found the *Bismarck*. But he had been forced to steer into the midst of his own mine field to escape her. And he feared that the *Bismarck*'s radar might have discovered him. If so, the radar could also give the German battleship the range, and that would be the end of the *Suffolk*. Frantically—before it might be too late—the Captain sent out a radio message that he had sighted the *Bismarck*. Further messages in rapid succession gave her position, course and speed.

Captain Phillips on the *Norfolk* was just having dinner when a signal petty officer broke into his cabin in high excitement.

"*Suffolk*'s got 'em, sir!" he cried.

The electrifying news crackled over the air waves to the other ships of the navy and to the Admiralty in London. The *Bismarck* had been found! The next job for the British was to engage her and sink her.

Back in the mist Captain Ellis aboard the *Suffolk* watched the *Bismarck* and her companion cruiser on his radar screen. He let them pass him and then, at a distance of some fifteen miles, emerged from the fog and began shadowing them. The *Norfolk* also changed course to join in the chase. But when the British cruiser suddenly emerged from the mist her captain saw the German battleship and cruiser only six miles away, steering directly for him. Captain Phillips turned sharply to starboard and immediately made a smoke screen to hide behind while speeding for the protection of the fog.

Too late! This time the lookouts on the *Bismarck* had their eyes open. The German battleship opened fire on the British cruiser with her 15-inch guns. Three salvos straddled the smaller ship and another narrowly missed her. Splinters rained down on the *Norfolk*'s deck but she escaped unharmed into the mist.

Admiral Luetjens aboard the *Bismarck* now knew he had been found. But as the arctic half-night fell and the weather worsened he believed that he might be able to shake off his shadowers. It began to snow hard and visibility declined to one mile. Toward midnight the *Suffolk*'s radar lost contact with the enemy ships. An hour went by, and another, and still no contact. The *Bismarck* was again lost. The spirits of the men on the British ships sank. Then at 2:50 A.M., on May 24, which was to be a fateful day, the *Suffolk* regained touch with the *Bismarck* on her radar screen. At 3:20 A.M., as the visibility improved, Captain Ellis resighted the German ship twelve miles ahead on his port bow.

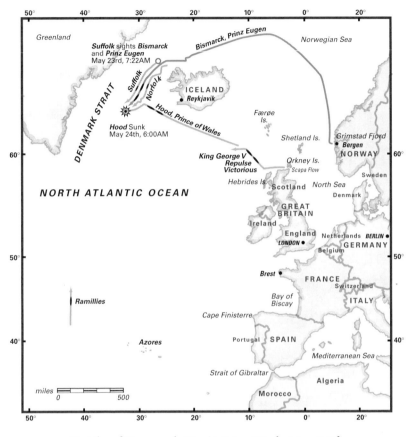

Battle of Denmark Strait, May 23rd–May 24th

All through the stormy, snowy night Captain Ellis had kept the ships of the British Fleet informed by radio of the ups and downs of his shadowing. He gave the position, course and speed of the *Bismarck* whenever he could spot her.

27

Shortly after eight o'clock on the evening of May 23, Vice-Admiral Holland, aboard the *Hood*, had picked up the first signal that the *Bismarck* had been found. He calculated that his battle squadron was some 300 miles due south of the Germans and he changed course to meet them head on. At midnight he ordered the crews of the *Hood* and the *Prince of Wales* to their action stations. But when word came a few minutes later that the *Suffolk* had lost contact with the enemy, the Admiral relaxed his orders. Crews were told they could snatch some sleep at their action stations.

The news that the *Bismarck* had been relocated reached the *Hood*'s squadron at 3:00 A.M. Vice-Admiral Holland realized that he was now near the enemy, and he gave orders to close in at full speed—twenty-eight knots. By 4:00 A.M. he estimated he was within twenty miles. Visibility was increasing with the coming of daylight. By 4:30 A.M. it was up to twelve miles and improving. Any moment now the German *Bismarck* might heave in sight. At 5:10 A.M. Admiral Holland signaled instant readiness for action. Twenty-five minutes later—at 5:35 A.M.—his lookouts saw on the distant horizon off the starboard beam the silhouettes of two German warships.

The moment the British navy had been waiting for so impatiently had come. It was a moment that Admiral Luetjens on the *Bismarck* had hoped to avoid. His orders were to sink British merchant shipping and evade battle with the British navy if he could. That was no longer possible. Two British capital ships were converging on him at top speed. One was certainly the *Hood*, which he knew to be the most powerful warship in the British navy. The other, he decided must be the new battleship *King George V*, though actually it was the sister ship, *Prince of Wales*.

Despite the fact that he was outgunned by the British ships, Admiral Luetjens did not flinch. At 5:52 A.M. he radioed Berlin: "Am engaging two heavy units."

At that very moment the 15-inch guns of the *Hood* went off at a range of 25,000 yards (over 14 miles!). The 14-inch guns of the *Prince of Wales* opened fire a few seconds later. Immediately the *Bismarck* replied with a broadside from her 15-inch guns. The German cruiser *Prinz Eugen* joined in with her own 8-inch cannon.

A great naval battle was engaged in the icy, northern sea.

CHAPTER 3

FIRST BATTLE: THE *BISMARCK* SINKS THE *HOOD*

THE BATTLE WAS ALL OVER IN EXACTLY SEVENTEEN MINUTES.

At the outset Vice-Admiral Holland ordered the *Hood* to fire at the wrong ship. He mistook the German cruiser *Prinz Eugen* for the battleship *Bismarck* and directed the opening 15-inch gun salvos of his flagship against the smaller enemy vessel.

The captain of the *Prince of Wales* realized the mistake at once and disregarded the Admiral's signal to follow suit. Instead he aimed his 14-inch guns immediately at the *Bismarck*. But his turrets were new and untried and his first shots landed wide of the target.

Vice Admiral Lancelot Ernest Holland

Vice-Admiral Holland had put his two battleships at a disadvantage from the moment the engagement began. Two minutes after sighting the German squadron he had turned his ships directly toward the enemy to shorten the range. The result was that the four rear guns on each of the British ships could not fire. Only the fore turrets, pointing toward the Germans, could be used.

Admiral Luetjens, on the other hand, steered a course so that all of his eight heavy guns could bear on the enemy. Had the British ships turned their full broadsides on him, they would have had the advantage of eighteen big guns against his eight. (There were ten guns on the *Prince of Wales* and eight on the *Hood*.) As it was, only the six forward cannon of the *Prince of Wales* and the four of the

Hood could be employed. This reduced the British advantage to only ten heavy guns against the Germans' eight, and after the first shot one of the *Prince of Wales'* forward guns was unable to fire further. Thus Vice-Admiral Holland's superiority was reduced to a mere nine to eight.

Since the German gunnery proved to be much more accurate than the British, this was not much of an advantage. In fact, not only the *Bismarck* but also the much smaller *Prinz Eugen*, with guns of only 8-inch caliber, soon found the range. Concentrating her fire on the *Hood*, the *Prinz Eugen* scored a hit in less than a minute with an 8-inch shell. It caused a large fire to break out near the *Hood*'s mainmast. Observers on the British cruisers *Suffolk* and *Norfolk* saw the flames spread forward and leap high above the upper deck. Then the fire seemed to subside.

The pair of shadowing British cruisers which had found the *Bismarck* were holding back to let the British battleships finish her. They took no part in the battle. Why they were not directed to join in remains a mystery. With the *Bismarck* and *Prinz Eugen* fully occupied by the British heavy ships, why did not Vice-Admiral Holland instruct the *Suffolk* and *Norfolk* to move in from the opposite quarter and engage the Germans with their 8-inch guns? The

Prinz Eugen's 8-inch guns had drawn first blood against the mighty *Hood*. Also the British cruisers might have launched torpedoes against the foe. But throughout the brief battle the *Suffolk* and *Norfolk* remained aloof.

The HMS *Hood*

Disaster now struck swiftly at the British. Both sides had opened fire at 5:52 A.M. Three minutes later Vice-Admiral Holland finally gave the order to his two ships to turn 20 degrees to port away from the Germans. This would enable them to employ their aft guns and fire broadsides at the enemy from all their big cannon.

The move came too late. As the British ships veered

around, a salvo from the *Bismarck* hit the *Hood* midships. Observers on both sides saw a scene they had never before looked upon at sea. Between the two funnels of the *Hood* there was suddenly a volcanic flame that erupted skyward for a thousand feet. Then in a second or two it burned out, and a dense cloud of smoke settled over the seas. For a moment the wind seemed to part it and through the smoke could be seen the severed bow and stern of the great ship jutting high in the sea, like two mammoth sharks. Then they sank below the waves.

The *Hood* had blown up.

Every high officer in the British navy had known that the mighty battle cruiser had an Achilles heel. There was a chink in its armor between the funnels. Years before the Admiralty had decided to correct this, but for one reason or another the job had been postponed. Then the war had come, and there was no time.

Thus it was that at precisely four minutes to six o'clock on the morning of May 24, 1941, just four minutes after the battle had begun, a 15-inch shell from the *Bismarck* hit the *Hood* in its weakest spot. It pierced through half a dozen decks to the magazine, where it exploded among 300 tons of high-explosive shells.

HMS *Hood* photographed from the *Prince of Wales*

Out of a crew of 1,419 only three men were picked up alive. Vice-Admiral Holland, Captain Ralph Kerr and all the rest went down with the ship.

CHAPTER 4

"AVENGE THE *HOOD*!"

THE SINKING OF THE *HOOD* PLUNGED THE BRITISH ISLES into deep gloom. The seafaring nation, whose navy had ruled the waves for so long, had suffered a bitter defeat at sea.

There were cries from high and low that the *Hood* be avenged. At once! But the prospects were not high. For after the *Hood* blew up, the battle had continued to go badly for the British.

On disposing so quickly of the *Hood*, the *Bismarck* and the *Prinz Eugen* had turned their undivided attention to the smaller surviving British battleship, the *Prince of Wales*. For five minutes the *Prince of Wales* had been firing away at the *Bismarck* undisturbed. Because she was so new that civilian mechanics were still working on her gun turrets, her firing had not been very accurate. And there had been several breakdowns. One gun was completely out. Others could be fired only with difficulty.

With the *Hood* gone, the *Prince of Wales* now received a murderous hail of fire from the two German warships. One 15-inch shell smashed her bridge, killing or wounding everyone on it except the captain and a signal man. The ship's side was pierced by several hits both below and above the water line. Several compartments were flooded. All the time the *Prince of Wales* continued to fire defiantly with what guns she could.

But it was an unequal struggle. For some reason the cruisers *Suffolk* and *Norfolk* were not joining in, as was the German cruiser. Captain Leach therefore decided to withdraw—at least momentarily. He knew that strong reinforcements were not far away. So at 6:03 A.M., just eleven minutes after the battle had begun, the *Prince of Wales* turned sharply around and retired behind her own thick smoke screen. The *Bismarck* fired a parting salvo at her six minutes later. The astonishing German victory had been won in exactly seventeen minutes.

The German admiral now made his first mistake. He failed to follow the crippled *Prince of Wales* and dispatch her as he had the *Hood*. Instead he resumed course southwest toward the mid-Atlantic.

After such a resounding triumph, why did Admiral Luetjens not pursue the damaged British battleship, sink her and then turn back to Germany? There he and his crews would have been hailed as victors, and Nazi propaganda could have made the most of it. The blow to British prestige would have been all the stronger. In Berlin Adolf Hitler, the Nazi German dictator, posed the question to Grand Admiral Erich Raeder, commander in chief of the German navy.

Admiral Luetjens had a good reason for continuing on, as was later learned from the secret German naval records. Though the British did not yet know it, the *Bismarck* had been hit by the *Prince of Wales*. Because of that, the Admiral made a decision which was to be fateful for both sides. At one minute past eight o'clock on the eventful morning of May 24, he informed Berlin in a coded radio message:

1. Electric engine room No. 4 broken down.
2. Port boiler room No. 2 is making water, but can be held. Water in the forecastle.
3. Maximum speed 28 knots.

4. Two enemy radar sets recognized.
5. Intentions: to put into St. Nazaire.
   No losses of personnel.

Fleet Commander

It seems a reasonable decision, considering all the circumstances. The *Bismarck* was crippled, though not badly. If Admiral Luetjens turned back through the Denmark Strait, he might run head on into the rest of the British Home Fleet. If the weather cleared, he would be subject nearly all the way to attack from British bombers based in Iceland and the northern British islands. Probably the German Fleet Commander calculated too that the British had no heavy ships between him and refuge at St. Nazaire on the French coast. On the way in he might knock off a British convoy or two. (As a matter of fact, the British convoy WS8B with 20,000 troops was almost directly in his path.)

Furthermore, at St. Nazaire, Admiral Luetjens would find his old battle cruisers *Scharnhorst* and *Gneisenau*. As soon as repairs were completed on them and on the *Bismarck*, he could then sally out to sea again with an even more formidable fleet.

There was a sharp argument between the Admiral and

Captain Lindemann, skipper of the *Bismarck*. The latter, a determined man who was very popular with his crew, advised turning back. A few minutes earlier he had urged in vain that they pursue the *Prince of Wales* (which they still believed was the *King George V*) and sink her. Now again his advice was rejected. The German admiral ordered the course southwest to be continued.

It was a command that would lead him to disaster.

While the cruisers *Suffolk* and *Norfolk*, followed by the battered *Prince of Wales*, hung on to the *Bismarck* after the battle, the British Admiralty mobilized a powerful armada to avenge the *Hood*. "Sink the *Bismarck*!" was the watchword. And from all over the wide Atlantic His Majesty's warships began to converge on the German man-of-war.

Sir John Tovey, commander in chief of the Home Fleet, had been some 500 miles southeast of the *Bismarck* when she was first spotted in the Denmark Strait. From Admiral Holland's reports, he had expected that the *Hood*'s squadron would intercept the German battleship about dawn. And he had waited confidently and calmly for the news of the meeting. When it came, he was shocked, as was every other British officer who heard the news. But the bitter blow only increased his resolution to get the enemy battleship. He therefore set an interception course for his flagship, *King George V*, with the battle cruiser *Repulse* and the carrier *Victorious* following in line astern. With luck, they thought they might meet the *Bismarck* at about dawn the next day.

BISMARCK CAPTAIN
ERNST LINDEMANN

But these were not the only British warships on the move. As soon as the *Bismarck* was sighted, the Admiralty had quickly ordered Force H at Gibraltar to speed out into the Atlantic. This fleet was under the command of Vice-Admiral Sir James Somerville and consisted of the battle cruiser *Renown*—sister ship of the *Repulse*—the carrier *Ark Royal*, the 6-inch-gun cruiser *Sheffield* and six destroyers.

The initial objective of Somerville's fleet was to race to the protection of Troop Convoy WS8B, now well out to sea and bound for the Middle East. Detaching the *Repulse* and the carrier *Victorious* from the convoy's original escort in order to strengthen Admiral Tovey's squadron had left the troop convoy virtually unprotected. With the *Bismarck* at large, it was in a precarious position. The navy could take no chance of losing 20,000 troops at sea.

But as soon as the *Hood* was sunk, the navy desperately decided to take a chance. The Admiralty directed Admiral Somerville to abandon the convoy and proceed at high speed toward the *Bismarck*.

Some 500 miles off the Irish coast the battleship *Rodney* was escorting the liner *Britannic* to America. The *Rodney*, with her 16-inch guns, was a powerful ship, but she was badly in need of repairs. One of her engine rooms kept breaking down. In fact she was scheduled to put into Boston for refitting. Her decks were piled high with replacement materials. She was also jammed with 500 war invalids for Canada.

Her commander, Captain Dalrymple-Hamilton, realized he was scarcely in a position to do battle with the most powerful warship afloat. Nevertheless, shortly after noon on May 24 he received orders to leave the *Britannic* and make full speed for the *Bismarck*.

Far to the southwest the battleship *Ramillies* was instructed to abandon her convoy, HX127, in the mid-Atlantic and steam at top speed to converge on the *Bismarck*. Two other cruisers, somewhere between the Azores and England, were also brought in on the chase.

It was a chase unique in modern naval history. Over a million square miles of stormy ocean three British battleships, two battle cruisers, two aircraft carriers and numerous cruisers and destroyers were steaming at full speed toward the *Bismarck* and the *Prinz Eugen*. Six hours earlier, their commanders and crews had learned by radio of the fate of the *Hood*. They were grimly determined to avenge her.

CHAPTER 5

THE *BISMARCK* IS LOST

THE GERMANS WERE MAKING THEIR PLANS TOO. At a quarter to two on the afternoon of May 24, Admiral Luetjens radioed naval headquarters in Berlin. After giving the *Bismarck*'s position he reported:

> *King George* with cruiser is maintaining contact. If no engagement, intend to attempt to shake off enemy during night.
>
> Fleet Commander

A few minutes later he sent a message to Berlin elaborating on his plan.

> Intend to shake off enemy as follows: During rain showers *Bismarck* will move off on westerly course.

Prinz Eugen to maintain course . . . Following this she
is to oil from *Belchen* or *Lothringen* and afterwards to
engage in cruiser warfare independently . . .

Fleet Commander

Twenty minutes later the Admiral got off a third message
about another plan. This was addressed to German submarines in the north-central Atlantic. He ordered them to
assemble at a point south of him and to be there by dawn.
He explained that he was approaching from the north and
intended to draw the British heavy units shadowing him
into this area.

The plan of the German admiral was for his two ships to
separate. The *Bismarck* would elude her pursuers during
the night, but in so doing she would lure the shadowing
British warships into a German U-boat trap.

Actually this was exactly what Admiral Tovey on his
flagship *King George V* feared. As the evening of May 24
approached, he was concerned that the *Bismarck* might
put on high speed during the night and give him the slip.
At the same time he might well be drawn into a nest of
U-boats. His squadron was still some 200 miles almost due
east of the German battleship.

But the cruisers *Suffolk* and *Norfolk* and the damaged

Prince of Wales were still hanging on to her, just out of range. It was an increasingly difficult task in the foul weather. Several times during the afternoon one or the other of the shadowing cruisers lost sight of the *Bismarck* in the fog and mist. And there were anxious periods when the *Suffolk* could not even maintain contact with radar.

The commanders of the two cruisers had to be careful. Any moment the *Bismarck*, lost from sight in the fog, might turn suddenly on them and blow them out of the sea. Actually at 6:30 P.M. the German battleship made just such a maneuver.

On his radar screen, Captain Ellis suddenly saw the speck that represented the *Bismarck* coming at him full speed. He could not see the enemy ship but he could spot her on his radar. Fearing an ambush he turned quickly to port. But, as he swung around, the *Bismarck* appeared out of the mist at only 20,000 yards. Captain Ellis ordered a smoke screen to be made. But before he could disappear behind it the *Bismarck* opened fire on him. Luckily her first shots were wide, and the *Suffolk* soon steamed full speed out of range.

The crippled *Prince of Wales*, in the meantime,

Bismarck firing on HMS *Prince of Wales* in the Battle of Denmark Strait

opened fire with what guns she had, and a second battle between the two big ships seemed underway. But the *Bismarck*, after unlimbering a few shots, hauled off out of range.

Why? ... The *Bismarck* had simply turned and opened fire on her pursuers in order to mask the getaway of the *Prinz Eugen*. Once that had been successfully accomplished she resumed course. She did not want to battle a British battleship in her present condition.

The British, however, knew nothing of her wounds. Not even the *Bismarck*'s avoiding battle that late afternoon made them suspicious. In fact they had assumed, after the sinking of the *Hood*, that the *Bismarck* had not been hit. Here, as so often during this drama on the high seas, a human error had played a role.

Actually, one of the two shells from the *Prince of Wales* which hit the *Bismarck* had penetrated deep down. It had exploded among some of her oil tanks and blown a hole in the ship's side. This had not only let water into the damaged tanks, making the oil useless for fuel, but had resulted in a leak of oil. Soon afterward both the cruiser *Suffolk* and a British Sunderland flying boat arriving on the scene from Iceland observed that the German ship was leaving a heavy track of oil behind her.

The *Suffolk* signaled this interesting discovery to the *Norfolk*, but the latter ship failed to get the message. Then the flying boat, circling above the *Bismarck*, radioed the *Norfolk*: "Losing oil." But since the plane had been under the *Bismarck*'s anti-aircraft fire, the captain of the *Norfolk* assumed that it was the aircraft which was losing oil. Not until late in the afternoon did a report reach the various British ships from Iceland that the plane's crew had definitely seen the *Bismarck* leaving a carpet of oil in her wake.

Bismarck vanishes, May 24th–May 25th

Even then Admiral Tovey did not take the report
seriously. A rather unimportant small leak, he knew, could
leave quite an oil track at sea. After all, the *Bismarck* had
been making good speed all day. There was every likeli-
hood that during the night she could even increase that
speed and have a good chance of getting away. Therefore

he must find some means of slowing up the German battleship before dark.

There was only one means of doing it—by torpedoes from the Swordfish planes aboard the carrier *Victorious*. Only by air could he get to the *Bismarck* and attempt to damage her. Sir John therefore ordered the *Victorious* to launch an attack with her torpedo-carrying planes. This could not be done until the carrier was within one hundred miles of the enemy since the range of the planes was very limited. Admiral Tovey calculated that the carrier would reach that point at about 9:00 P.M.—in the very last hours of the fading daylight.

This meant that after the attack the inexperienced pilots would probably have to land on the carrier deck in the darkness—a tricky feat that none of them had ever attempted before. Still, it was this attack by air, or nothing. The risk had to be taken. And it was.

The *Victorious* did not get within striking distance until after 10:00 P.M. Her nine planes were clocked off the flight deck at 10:30 P.M. Little more than two hours remained before sunset. (Because the British navy operated by double summer time and because of the position in the mid-Atlantic, the ships' clocks were actually about four hours ahead of actual sun time. Sunset, by this reckoning, would not come until 12:52 A.M.).

After an hour's flight the Swordfish pilots sighted what they thought was the *Bismarck* about twenty miles away. But when they flew over the *Norfolk*, on the way to close in, the British cruiser signaled frantically that they were flying in the wrong direction. She gave them the correct bearings, and they again formed for the torpedo attack. Keeping cover in the clouds, they closed in on their target, which they could see on their radar screens.

But when they swooped down into the clear again to loose their torpedoes, they discovered that the target was neither the *Bismarck* nor any British ship. It was a mysterious vessel which apparently neither the German nor the British ships had noticed. Actually, as they learned much later, it was the United States Coast Guard Cutter *Modoc*, out on neutrality patrol.

The *Bismarck*, however, was not far away. Her lookouts saw the little Swordfish planes and gave the alarm. Thus when the torpedo-carrying aircraft finally attacked, the Germans were ready for them with their anti-aircraft guns. Though the German fire was murderous, the Swordfish pilots pressed home their attack, skimming in just above the waves to launch their torpedoes against the German warship. They saw one torpedo hit home and explode.

In the meantime the *Norfolk* had sighted the USCG *Modoc* and in the poor visibility mistook her for the *Bismarck*. The British cruiser turned sharply away. As she did so, Rear-Admiral Wake-Walker signaled the *Prince of Wales* to open fire on the *Modoc*. Fortunately for the American vessel there was a momentary mechanical failure aboard the *Prince of Wales*. By the time it was fixed, the *Modoc* had slipped out of sight. By this narrow margin, she escaped being blown out of the sea!

It was dark, and raining hard before the planes, returning from the attack, approached their carrier. Aboard the *Victorious* there were anxious faces. Not one of the pilots had ever before landed at night on a carrier deck. To add to their difficulties the ship's homing beacon, by which the planes were usually guided in at night, would not function.

In desperation Captain H. C. Bovell, commander of the carrier, switched on his bright searchlights. An order to shut them off came immediately from the vice-admiral in command of the escorting cruisers of the Home Fleet. The searchlights were endangering the whole fleet. Captain

Bovell kept them on until a second order that brooked no disobedience came to him. But the pilots had seen the lights. All of the Swordfish, miraculously, put down safely on the dark, rain-swept deck.

Aboard the *Bismarck*, Admiral Luetjens had radioed brief messages in code to Berlin telling of the air attack.

23:38. [11:38 P.M.] Air attack in approximate position 56 50N, 36 20W.
00:28. [12:28 A.M. of May 25] Attack by carrier-borne aircraft. Torpedo hit starboard.
01:53. Torpedo hit of no importance.

Aboard the *King George V*, Admiral Tovey had been cheered by the reports that the Swordfish planes from the *Victorious* had found the *Bismarck* despite the miserable weather and the failing light. He felt even better when the signal came in that one torpedo hit had been observed. This might well slow up the *Bismarck* and give him the chance for which he had been waiting so long: to close in and engage her. Hopefully, but not without impatience, he waited for confirmation from the *Suffolk* and *Norfolk* that the *Bismarck*'s speed had been reduced. Trailing her as they were, they would soon know.

Past midnight, past 1:00 A.M. and on to two o'clock, Admiral Tovey waited expectantly. No news came of any slowing up of the *Bismarck*. She seemed to be steaming on at the same speed as before.

Somewhat depressed, the Admiral decided to turn in for a nap. It had been a rough and discouraging day for him. At dawn he had in lost the *Hood* the most powerful battleship in the fleet. And one of the two newest of his battleships, the *Prince of Wales*, had been damaged, though it was still in the chase. His ships had not given a very good account of themselves. So far as he knew, they had not damaged the *Bismarck* seriously, if at all. Her guns seemed as fit as ever, her speed undiminished.

Even if he could intercept her the next day, which now seemed doubtful, his own fleet would be further weakened. At midnight he had had to send his destroyers back to Iceland to refuel. This left him without destroyer protection at the very moment he was entering U-boat-infested waters. His battle cruiser *Repulse* would have to leave him by nine the next morning. She would have just enough fuel to get back to port. And there was little chance that he could corner the enemy battleship by so early an hour.

Shortly after he turned in for a nap, the Admiral was awakened by further bad news. At six minutes past three o'clock on May 25, while the night was still black, and the weather miserable with mist and rain, the *Suffolk* lost contact with the *Bismarck*.

The ships of both sides had begun zigzagging during the night because of the possibility of the presence of German submarines. (Admiral Luetjens could not be sure that one of his own submarines might not mistake his ship for a British vessel in the darkness.) On one of the outward zigzags away from the *Bismarck*, the *Suffolk* had lost contact on her radar. She did not regain it on her inward zigzag.

Captain Ellis on the *Suffolk*, numb from the cold and lack of sleep, increased speed. He had been on the bridge almost continuously for four days and nights. A blast from one of his own guns had shattered the protective glass on the bridge, leaving it exposed to the icy winds. And now for an hour he plunged forward at full steam, seeking to regain contact with the enemy. At 4:00 A.M. he ruefully signaled the Home Fleet: "Have lost contact with the *Bismarck*. Am making a search."

When Admiral Tovey heard the news, he hastened to

the chart room to ponder it with his staff. There was no denying that this was a blow. After thirty-one and a half hours of skillful and persistent shadowing, the British had let the enemy slip away.

The mighty *Bismarck* was lost!

CHAPTER 6

WHERE IS THE *BISMARCK*?

LOSS OF CONTACT WITH THE *BISMARCK* CAUSED THE British government in London, as Prime Minister Winston Churchill later admitted, the "utmost anxiety."

For Admiral Tovey, whose fleet had got within a hundred miles of the enemy and then lost her, there were a number of urgent questions to try to answer on that morning of May 25.

Had the *Bismarck* turned west toward Greenland to meet a German tanker for refueling? Had she turned south for a rendezvous with a tanker near the Azores, or southeast for repairs at Brest or St. Nazaire on the French coast? Or had she perhaps turned back for the Denmark Strait whence she could continue home to bases in Norway and Germany?

After considering all the possibilities, Sir John chose the first two: that the *Bismarck* was steering either west for Greenland or south for the Azores in order to refuel. He directed the cruisers *Suffolk* and *Norfolk* to cover the west and northwest courses. He ordered the carrier *Victorious* to send planes on an aerial search in that general direction. Her protecting cruisers were to accompany her. The battle cruiser *Repulse* was now so short of oil that she was instructed to leave the squadron and proceed to Newfoundland for refueling. On the way, she would be in a position to cover the western search area.

The battleship *Ramillies* was some 400 miles to the south and steaming almost due north. She was told to continue on course. She was old and slow and hardly able to stand up to the *Bismarck* should they meet alone. But she was all the British had at the moment to engage the German battleship if she had veered south toward the Azores.

Sir John himself turned southwest with what was left of his Home Fleet. Not much was left. His battle cruiser and carrier, as well as his cruisers and destroyers, were gone.

His one remaining battleship, the *King George V*, was scarcely a match for the more powerful *Bismarck*, so he ordered her sister ship, the *Prince of Wales*, to join him. Though crippled, the *Prince of Wales* had doggedly remained in the search with the *Suffolk* and *Norfolk*. She now left them to join Admiral Tovey's flagship.

There were other heavy British ships which might play a vital role if the *Bismarck* were found again. The chief of these was the battleship *Rodney*. Although the *Rodney*, as we have seen, was badly in need of repairs, her commander was sure she could put up a good fight if necessary.

All night long the *Rodney* had been steaming at full speed to join Admiral Tovey. About 3:00 A.M. on the 25th, when her destroyer escort began to fall behind in the rough seas, Captain Dalrymple-Hamilton pushed his battleship on alone, leaving his destroyers to catch up as best they could.

When he learned two hours later that the *Bismarck* had been lost, the *Rodney* was about 400 miles southeast of the German ship's last known position. This, the captain saw at once, was a pretty good place in which to be. He was sure that the *Bismarck* was now making for a French or Spanish port for repairs. If so, the *Rodney* was almost directly in her way. The wisest course, therefore, was for Captain Dalrymple-Hamilton to stop and remain just about where he was. And that is what he did.

Vice-Admiral Somerville's Force H—including the battle cruiser *Renown*, the aircraft carrier *Ark Royal* and the cruiser *Sheffield*—was still more than a thousand miles to the southeast. All it could do for the moment was to continue at full speed to the northwest. At first it seemed to Somerville that he had left Gibraltar too late to get in on any action. But then it began to occur to him that, if the *Bismarck* made for a Spanish or French port, he might still join the fight. He pressed on as fast as he could.

Unlike Somerville and Captain Dalrymple-Hamilton, the Commander in Chief of the Home Fleet did not believe that the lost *Bismarck* was heading southeast toward Spain or France. All morning long—from 6:30 A.M. until nearly eleven o'clock—Admiral Tovey steered southwestward, searching in vain for the vanished enemy.

Then the British had a stroke of luck. Admiral Luetjens broke radio silence!

Early in the morning the Admiral had begun to send a series of coded radio messages to German naval headquarters reporting the *Bismarck*'s position and other information. The British were dumbfounded—but grateful. They could not decode the German admiral's figures giving his latitude and longitude. But they could determine his position fairly accurately by means of radio direction-finding stations in Britain and Northern Ireland.

Why did the crafty and experienced German admiral take such a risk? Not one of his messages was urgent, or even necessary. We discovered this after the war when the contents of the messages became available from the German naval archives. Why did he send them and risk giving away his position when the whole British navy was vainly searching for a trace of him?

Here again a human error crept in. Admiral Luetjens didn't know the British had lost him! He thought he was still being shadowed. Indeed, in the very first radio message sent at 7:27 on the morning of May 25 he stated: "One battleship and two heavy cruisers maintaining contact." He had no idea that the "one battleship" (*Prince of Wales*) and the "two heavy cruisers" (*Suffolk* and *Norfolk*) had completely lost him more than four hours before. So he continued to send off his radio messages. And the British direction finding radio stations continued to get a fix on him.

Then Admiral Luetjens had a stroke of luck. This, too,

was due to a weird but human error—this time an error of the British. Aboard Admiral Tovey's flagship a mistake was made in simple arithmetic.

The British Admiralty in London had radioed the Admiral's ship at 10:30 A.M., giving the bearings on the *Bismarck* as received at 8:52 A.M. by their direction finding sets. For some unexplainable reason the Admiralty failed to give the position of the *Bismarck* as it had been plotted from the radio bearings. This was a costly piece of negligence.

But in the navigation room on the *King George V*, it was easy to plot the enemy's position from the bearings given. A navigation officer proceeded to do so. Perhaps he was in a hurry. It is said that his charts were not sufficiently detailed. Whatever the reason, he made a false mathematical calculation. This put the position of the *Bismarck* considerably to the *north* of where she had been when last seen on the *Suffolk's* radar at 3 o'clock A.M. Admiral Tovey was forced to concluded that the *Bismarck* had turned north in the darkness and was heading home. He immediately reversed course to northeast and advised all other search ships to steer accordingly.

At full speed Sir John's Home Fleet headed off in what turned out to be the wrong direction.

Two British warships declined to follow the orders of the commander in chief. Captain Dalrymple-Hamilton on the battleship *Rodney* concluded that if the *Bismarck* were really heading northeast he was too far south to catch her. But he was now sure in his seaman's bones that the German battleship was making for France. In that case the *Rodney* would be in her way. The Captain, therefore, against superior orders, remained where he was.

Rear Admiral Wake-Walker aboard the cruiser *Norfolk* also felt in his bones that the *Bismarck* must have turned toward Brest or St. Nazaire on the French coast. On his own—and also contrary to Admiral Tovey's orders—he set course in that general direction.

Force H, coming up from Gibraltar, was not under the direct command of Sir John. Vice-Admiral Somerville aboard the *Renown* received Admiral Tovey's orders for the new search northeast but he also disregarded them. He decided to follow instructions from the Admiralty, received shortly before, and assume that the *Bismarck* was heading for France.

In the Admiralty in London there was much confusion. No one at the nerve center of the British navy in London noticed that Admiral Tovey's plotting of the position of the

Bismarck was at variance to their own and that the Home Fleet obviously was going off on a mad chase in the wrong direction. As the hours passed, most of the top-ranking naval officers in London became certain that the *Bismarck* was making for France. Yet Admiral Tovey was not informed of this.

Finally, at 3:30 in the afternoon, Tovey received a radio message from the Admiralty giving a new position for the *Bismarck*. This had been plotted from radio directional bearings received from the enemy ship's radio two hours earlier.

Admiral Luetjens had continued to send out a stream of radio messages all day. The twenty-fifth of May was his birthday and he had received a number of birthday congratulations radioed from Berlin. Even Adolf Hitler, the Nazi dictator of Germany, had sent him a message: "Best wishes on your birthday."

It was perhaps only natural for the German admiral to reply—and thus by his radio broadcasts to unwittingly keep the British informed of his course and changing position. He still was sure he was being shadowed. There was no sense in maintaining radio silence when the enemy had his ship on its radar screen and knew exactly where he was.

At 8:46 A.M. Naval Group West, under whose command he now was, had radioed Luetjens that it believed he had given the slip to his pursuers.

> Last enemy contact report [it advised] was at 02:13 [2:13 A.M.]. We have impression that contact with *Bismarck* has been lost.

Unfortunately for himself, his ship and crew, the headstrong German admiral did not believe it. He still failed to believe it at 6:30 that evening when Group West again radioed him saying that there had been no British reports of sighting the *Bismarck* all day. Thus the mistakes on both sides were contributing to the sharpening of the tense drama now approaching its climax.

The position of the *Bismarck* radioed by the Admiralty to Sir John at 3:30 on the afternoon of May 25 came as a shock to the commander in chief. It showed that the enemy battleship was not heading north for home but southeast for a French port. It meant that Admiral Tovey had for several hours been engaged in a wild-goose chase in the wrong direction. Indeed, he realized that during the early afternoon the *Bismarck* must have passed him on her way south and now would have a head start in the race for the French coast.

Completely baffled, Admiral Tovey asked his navigation officer to check his arithmetic in the original plotting of the enemy's position. The officer did so and found his mistake. The German battleship had been pointing toward France all day!

At 6:10 P.M., Sir John, after waiting in vain for further word from the Admiralty, steered the Home Fleet around and set a new course southeast. An hour later the Admiralty approved. All British ships in the Atlantic, it ordered, were to try to intercept the *Bismarck* on her way to France.

The newly discovered course of the German vessel immediately put several British warships out of the race, for their fuel supplies were fast dwindling. The *Ramillies* had dropped out earlier in the day on receipt of the false news that the *Bismarck* had turned northeast. The old British battleship was much too slow to attempt to catch up on the new course. Therefore during the early afternoon the Admiralty had instructed her to take over the troopship *Britannic*, which the *Rodney* had had to abandon the day before. The *Ramillies* was to escort the *Britannic* on to Canada.

The cruiser *Suffolk*, which had turned west to look for the enemy off Greenland, was much too far away to join in the chase toward Brest. She now made for a refueling station in Iceland. So did the carrier *Victorious* and her escorting cruisers. The crippled *Prince of Wales* was also low on oil. She was ordered home. The *Norfolk*'s oil tanks were getting dangerously low. But Rear Admiral Wake-Walker decided to risk remaining in the chase with her.

The twenty-fifth of May had been another dark and frustrating day for Admiral Tovey. As evening came, with mounting seas, a stiff wind from the northwest and a falling barometer, he took stock of his situation.

He had hoped to give battle to the *Bismarck* at nine o'clock that morning. But during the hours of night just preceding she had been lost. Soon afterward he had had a stroke of luck when Admiral Luetjens broke radio silence. But because of a mistake in arithmetic on Tovey's own flagship, this good fortune had led him off on a wild-goose chase instead of bringing him into quick contact with the enemy.

As darkness fell over the stormy seas, he was alone. The once mighty Home Fleet had been reduced to one battleship, his flagship *King George V*. The *Hood* was lost. All the other war vessels had had to return to base to refuel. His own ship was dangerously low on oil. He had already had to reduce speed to conserve it. At reduced speed how could he catch and engage the *Bismarck*? He calculated that she was already at least 100 miles ahead of him and faster than his own ship.

The *Rodney* was somewhere in front of him, but just where Tovey did not know. Her captain, unlike the German admiral, had been observing radio silence all day.

And finally there was Force H, which had been coming up full steam from Gibraltar. Within twenty-four hours or so he ought to meet her. The more the commander in chief thought about it on that grim, stormy evening the more he saw that Vice-Admiral Somerville's squadron was probably his last and only hope. It stood between the *Bismarck* and safe refuge at Brest or St. Nazaire.

The battle cruiser *Renown* could scarcely be expected to stand up to the more powerful German battleship. But planes from the carrier *Ark Royal* might slow her up with torpedoes.

Of course the planes from the carrier *Victorious* had not been very successful in a similar attempt the night before.

Still, this was about his only hope. The torpedo-carrying Swordfish from the *Ark Royal* would at least have to reduce the speed of the *Bismarck* if Admiral Tovey were to catch her.

But first the enemy battleship had to be found. Sir John had a general idea of her whereabouts from the radio direction finders. But she had not been sighted by eye or radar since the night before. She must now be found or the chase was up.

For this, too, the scouting planes of the *Ark Royal* seemed to be his last hope. But unknown to the troubled British admiral there was still another source of hope.

CHAPTER 7

THE *BISMARCK* IS FOUND AGAIN!

ALL DAY LONG ON MAY 25 AND FAR INTO THE NIGHT three Catalinas from the Northern Ireland base had been out over the distant sea searching for the *Bismarck*.

Shortly after midnight one of them had sighted what looked in the murky night like a battleship and four destroyers. The big ship did not respond to the plane's signals. She could have been the *Bismarck*. And then again she might have been the *King George V*. In the black stormy night the pilot could not tell.

The three long-range flying boats did not get back to base until nearly noon on May 26 after almost twenty-four hours in the air. Long before that, two other flying boats of

Coastal Command from the same base in Northern Ireland had set out to join in the search. They had taken off from Lough Erne at 3:00 A.M. while the night was still black.

Catalina airplane of the type that located the *Bismarck*

The area they were to search had at last been strictly defined. This was a "square" some 700 miles due west of Brest. It was based partly on the positions of the *Bismarck* as plotted by the British radio direction-finding stations, taking into consideration her probable course and speed. It was also based, in part, on one man's hunch.

This man was Air Marshal Sir Frederick Bowhill, commander in chief of the R.A.F. Coastal Command.

Bowhill had been an officer in both the merchant marine and the navy before becoming a flier in the Royal Air Force. He thus knew the sea as well as the air—a rare quality in any airman.

From the moment news was received that the *Bismarck* was lost, Sir Frederick had had a hunch about what she was up to. She was making for Brest or St. Nazaire. Several naval officers at the Admiralty and on the ships at sea had had the same feeling. But Bowhill's hunch was something special.

He was sure that the German battleship would not head directly for the French ports. Rather, he thought, she would follow a wide circle. She would steer first for Cape Finisterre on the northwest coast of Spain. Since Spain was neutral, the Cape's lighthouse was still functioning. (The lights along the coasts of France and England were extinguished during the war as a measure of self-protection against hostile ships and planes.) Then, the Air Marshal reasoned, the *Bismarck* would proceed around the Bay of Biscay to haven at St. Nazaire or Brest.

On the evening of May 25, when Bowhill conferred with the Admiralty, he insisted on being allowed to follow his hunch. One of the two Catalinas must cover an assumed course of the *Bismarck* toward Cape Finisterre in Spain.

After some argument the Admiralty gave in to him on condition that the second plane search farther north on an assumed course of the enemy directly toward Brest. The square of search thus became a rectangle tilted northeast. It was about two hundred miles long and a hundred miles wide. It lay some 600 miles northwest of Cape Finisterre and 700 miles due west of Brest. If the *Bismarck* were making for either place, Bowhill calculated, she ought to be somewhere within the rectangle by 10:00 A.M. on May 26.

It was a rather large area for just two planes to cover, and the weather reports were discouraging. There were high winds and low clouds over mountainous seas. The Catalinas would have to get down low to discover any ships. And identification in such conditions of bad visibility would not be easy. Still, Sir Frederick was fairly optimistic as his two aircraft skimmed over the waters of Lough Erne, rose into the air and headed southwest into the darkness before dawn.

As daylight broke on May 26, Force H was getting close

to the prey. But closing in on the *Bismarck* was not the only problem faced by Vice-Admiral Somerville aboard his flagship *Renown*. He had another. Ever since steaming out of Gibraltar on the night of the 23rd he had been concerned about running into the German battle cruisers *Scharnhorst* and *Gneisenau*. On that day British planes had reported the two warships still in Brest, where they were undergoing repairs from a bombing by R.A.F. bombers some weeks before.

But after Somerville's squadron headed northward in the Atlantic, he received no more news about the two German ships. By May 25—two days later—the commander of Force H had to face the possibility that the *Scharnhorst* and *Gneisenau* might well have completed their repairs and put out from Brest to come to the rescue of the *Bismarck*. If so, they might be dangerously near his own squadron, which was no match for them.

Twice during May 25 as he sped toward the general direction of the *Bismarck*, Admiral Somerville had sent out aircraft from the carrier *Ark Royal* to look for the two German battle cruisers. But visibility had been so poor that the planes had been recalled shortly after taking off. In the evening the Admiral gave orders that the first dawn patrol of planes the next day would have to disregard the *Bismarck,* desperate as the search for her was. They must look first to see if the German battle cruisers were nearby.

The night of the 25th grew very stormy. So high were the waves that speed had to be drastically reduced—from twenty-six knots to twenty-three, and then down to nineteen and finally, just after midnight, to seventeen knots. At this rate, Somerville realized, he would never be able to converge on the *Bismarck.* And the high seas were threatening to smash up his ships. The small destroyers were barely able to keep afloat, and waves pounded over the decks of the cruiser *Sheffield* and the battle cruiser *Renown.*

Even the flight deck of the *Ark Royal,* sixty-three feet above the water line, was being washed by the heavy seas. Her bow and stern were rising and falling a distance of fifty-five feet as the ship pitched and rolled. If such seas kept on, the carrier would be unable to launch any planes at all from the lurching deck when the decisive time arrived.

The stormy seas were troubling the Germans too. Early on the afternoon of May 25, Naval Group West had radioed Admiral Luetjens that it was assembling seven U-boats to protect him on his run into Brest. At 7:32 P.M. it advised the German Fleet Commander that strong air forces also were being mobilized to give him protection and to bomb his pursuers. Three destroyers, it added, were putting out from Brest to join him.

But the seas were too high for them. Early on the morning of May 26 Naval Group West informed Admiral Luetjens by radio that the weather made it impossible for the destroyers to leave port. He would have to depend on "close air cover for the time being."

The truth was, as the German admiral realized, that he was still too far from land for the German bombers to be of any help to him. Even the longer-range German reconnaissance planes could not find the British pursuers in the low visibility of the storm. The *Bismarck* herself had had to reduce speed in the rough seas for fear of worsening the damage to her side and to her oil tanks.

Still, she was plowing along at twenty knots and her big guns were in tip-top shape. She had finally given the slip to the shadowing British ships. Admiral Luetjens realized this now. That enemy craft were still looking for him and might not be far off, he of course knew. But give him another few hours—until darkness of that day of May 26.

Then during the ensuing night he would arrive well within the protective cover of the famed Luftwaffe bombers and the U-boats. The German Fleet Commander, though by nature rather pessimistic, could not help but believe that he had a fairly good chance of escaping British detection during the rest of the daylight hours. The low clouds, the thick mist, the heavy seas would help cover him until night fell. Then the danger would be all but over. By daylight of May 27 he would be in safe waters.

His hopes were very shortly to be dashed.

At 7:00 A.M. on May 26 the *Ark Royal* sent out her dawn patrol. The scouting planes were to look for the German battle cruisers, *Scharnhorst* and *Gneisenau* coming out of Brest and for any U-boats that might be near. An hour and a half later ten Swordfish planes, minus their torpedoes, were brought up on the flight deck. At 8:35, after the carrier had turned into the wind, they began to take off in search of the *Bismarck*.

The *Ark Royal* was still tossing in the rough seas. It was touch-and-go whether the pilots would be able to get their little biplanes off the deck without cracking up or plunging into the waves. Vice-Admiral Somerville on the bridge of the *Renown* watched anxiously through his binoculars as the Swordfish careened off the pitching deck. To his relief, all got off safely. The aircraft had fuel for a three-and-a-half-hour search.

There now began for the men on the British ships a long and nerve-wracking wait. Somerville had radioed all the vessels in the area that the vital aerial search, on which they believed all now depended, had begun.

The *King George V* was some 300 miles to the northwest of Somerville's squadron, zigzagging southeast at 24 knots. On her port bow, but still out of sight, was the *Rodney* with three destroyers. Neither ship knew exactly where the other was because they had been observing radio silence. They calculated, however, that they were not far apart and sailing in pretty much the same course.

Both battleships took in Somerville's signal that he had launched ten planes from the *Ark Royal* to search for the *Bismarck* in an area between the two British naval forces. Admiral Tovey aboard the *King George V*, Captain Dalrymple-Hamilton on the *Rodney*, and Captain L. E. H. Maund, the determined skipper of the *Ark Royal*, counted the minutes and waited nervously for some word from the scouting planes.

These British commanders would have agreed with Admiral Luetjens on one thing. If the *Bismarck* could not be located this day then she was safe. A great German naval victory would have been completed. With the *Hood* unavenged the British would have suffered a complete defeat—in fact, a disaster.

Nine o'clock came. Nine-thirty. Ten. There was no news at all from the searching planes. Soon they would have to turn back to refuel.

Then at 10:30 A.M. a British plane began transmitting a message by radio. Excited wireless operators on a dozen British ships began writing it down.

> ... ONE BATTLESHIP ... SIGHTED ... POSITION 49 30 NORTH ... 21 50 WEST ... STEERING 150 degrees [Roughly southeast by east] ... SPEED ... 20 KNOTS ...

One battleship! Was it the *Bismarck*? Admirals and captains went quickly to their chart rooms and marked the given position on their maps. So far as they knew no British battleship was in the immediate vicinity. It must be the *Bismarck*!

And what British aircraft had found her? The radio message did not come from any of the *Ark Royal*'s Swordfish

Bismarck is found, morning, May 26th

planes. Instead the sender identified his plane as "Z/209." That would be a Catalina—"Z" of the 209th Squadron, R.A.F. Coastal Command. It was one of the two flying boats which had been sent out that morning to make the long flight from Northern Ireland to the area of search.

It had been in the air over seven hours when, in the words of one of the pilots:

> "George" [the automatic pilot] was flying the aircraft at 500 feet when we saw a warship. I was in the second pilot's seat when the occupant of the seat beside me, an American, said: "What the devil's that?"
>
> I stared ahead and saw a dull black ship through the mist which curled above a very rough sea.
>
> "Looks like a battleship," he said.
>
> I said: "Better get closer. Go round its stern."
>
> I thought it might be the *Bismarck* because I could see no destroyers around the ship and I should have seen them had she been a British warship.

Actually, as we know, the *King George V* no longer had any destroyers with her. If the pilot had happened to see the British ship, he undoubtedly would have made her out to be the *Bismarck*. But luck was with the British this day.

The pilot continued his report:

> I left my seat, went to the wireless operator's table, grabbed a piece of paper and began to write out a signal.
>
> The second pilot had taken over from "George" and gone up to 1,500 feet into broken cloud.
>
> As we came round he must have slightly misjudged his position. Instead of coming up astern we found ourselves right over the ship in an open space between the clouds!

Two black puffs appeared outside the starboard wing tip. In a moment we were surrounded by black puffs. Stuff began to rattle against the hull. Some of it went through and a lot more made dents in it.

I scribbled: "End of message." and handed it to the wireless operator. . . .

It was this message, crackling over the air waves, that electrified the officers and crew of every British warship engaged in the chase which up to this fateful moment had been so frustrating.

And the message had come from one of the two planes which had been sent out as a result of Air Marshal Sir Frederick Bowhill's hunch. The Z/209 had flown the southerly course of search on Sir Frederick's gamble that the German battleship was steering first for Spain. And indeed the *Bismarck*'s position as reported at 10:30 A.M. on May 26 showed that Admiral Luetjens had kept on a direct course not for Brest, as the Admiralty had predicted, but for Cape Finisterre. This was what Sir Frederick had felt certain of all along.

Acting on his hunch had paid off. After being lost for thirty-one and a half hours, the *Bismarck* had been found again!

CHAPTER 8

THE BRITISH ATTACK THE WRONG SHIP!

SO INTENSE WAS THE *BISMARCK'S* ANTI-AIRCRAFT FIRE that the Catalina quickly ducked into the clouds to escape being blown to pieces. When it came out again it could find no trace of the German battleship.

The *Bismarck* was again lost. But this time she was not lost for long. Half an hour later, one of the reconnaissance planes from the *Ark Royal* sighted her. The pilot mistook her for a cruiser and reported her as such to his carrier. The pilot of a second Swordfish arriving on the scene ten minutes later was sure the vessel was a battleship.

Which was it: a battleship or a cruiser, the *Bismarck* or

the *Prinz Eugen*? On their return to the carrier the fliers were closely questioned by Captain Maund. They were not quite sure which German ship they had seen. Identification in the murky weather was not easy. From a distance the two German war vessels looked very much alike. In fact, two days earlier Vice-Admiral Holland on the *Hood* had mistaken the *Prinz Eugen* for the *Bismarck* and directed his first salvos on her. If a veteran naval officer of high rank who had spent most of his life at sea found it almost impossible to distinguish the German cruiser from the battleship, it was not surprising that airmen had some difficulty.

Vice-Admiral Somerville on the *Renown* impatiently signaled over to the carrier for definite word. Captain Maund replied that his pilots were not sure which ship they had seen. They rather thought it was the *Prinz Eugen*. Somerville asked what Captain Maund himself thought. Maund replied that he was certain it was the *Bismarck*. What was his evidence? He had none. But like Air Marshal Bowhill he had a strong hunch. It too proved right.

Early that afternoon other planes from the *Ark Royal* hovered over the phantom German warship and confirmed that it was the *Bismarck*.

Though the rediscovery of the *Bismarck* brought relief and joy to the British naval commanders, it also presented them with some serious problems.

Unfortunately the main British battleships, the *King George V* and the *Rodney*, were too far away from their intended prey. And they were the only ones which could engage the *Bismarck* in a gun battle. Admiral Tovey on the *King George V* calculated that the enemy ship had a lead on him of at least fifty miles if she steered directly for Brest. If the *Bismarck* veered southward toward the center of the Bay of Biscay, the lead was about 100 miles. Since the latter course was the one which would most quickly bring the German battleship within the cover of German shore-based bombers, she would very likely steer for it.

The problem that the British commander in chief faced was how to get at the *Bismarck* with his heavy guns before dawn the next day. By that time she would reach air cover from German bombers based on the French coast. He would have to catch up with her before dark, or risk losing her again in the night. But this was obviously impossible at the slow rate he was gaining on her. Admiral Tovey saw that his only chance was to drastically reduce the *Bismarck*'s speed.

He had only two means of accomplishing this. Neither was very promising. One was by a destroyer torpedo attack. The other was by an assault from the torpedo-carrying Swordfish of the *Ark Royal*. Torpedoes, in fact, represented his only hope. But he was experienced enough to know that a ship built as stoutly as the *Bismarck* could probably withstand several torpedo hits without losing much speed.

Admiral Tovey, knowing his commanders as he did, had no doubt that Vice-Admiral Somerville would launch a torpedo attack from his carrier as soon as he could. No specific orders from the commander in chief would be needed to spur him on. And none were given. Nor were any orders given to the commander of a destroyer squadron which had now turned at full speed toward the reported position of the *Bismarck*.

This particular commander the Germans knew well. And they did not like him. His name was Captain Philip Vian. On the night of February 16, 1940, he had taken his destroyer *Cossack* into a Norwegian fiord, boarded a German auxiliary supply ship, the *Altmark*, and liberated 300 British seamen who were being taken as prisoners of war to Germany. In the scuffle four Germans were killed and five wounded, with no British losses. The German navy was humiliated. Her admirals were furious. Captain Vian became their pet hate.

On the morning of May 24, when the *Hood* was sunk, Captain Vian had been well out to sea west of the British Isles. Still on his favorite *Cossack*, he was in command of five destroyers escorting Troop Convoy WS8B. This was all the protection the precious convoy of 20,000 British troops had. The battle cruiser *Repulse* and the carrier *Victorious*, which originally were to have escorted it, had been detached to strengthen Admiral Tovey's squadron.

On the 25th, as the commander in chief searched desperately for the *Bismarck*, he became aware that his battleships *King George V* and *Rodney* were in dire danger of U-boat attacks because of their lack of destroyers. At 10:30 that night Admiral Tovey therefore sent an appeal to the Admiralty for an escort of these smaller ships.

The nearest destroyers to him, as it happened, were those of Captain Vian. Could the Admiralty risk detaching them from the troop convoy and sending them to protect Sir John's two battleships? If this were done, the ships of the convoy would be sitting ducks for a single German submarine. Twenty thousand British troops might be drowned in an hour. It was a hard decision to make. But it was made. Captain Vian was ordered to leave the convoy and steam at full speed north for the British battleships some 300 miles away. He began the dash at 2:00 A.M. on May 26.

When he heard, just before noon, that the Catalina had sighted an enemy battleship, the Captain was somehow sure that she must be the *Bismarck*. At that moment he was only about three hours' fast traveling time from a meeting with Admiral Tovey's battleships. Without waiting for fresh orders—indeed a violation of his standing orders to make a junction with Sir John's ships—Captain Vian turned around and dashed off at full speed through heavy seas with his five destroyers toward the enemy. He knew he could get to the *Bismarck* well ahead of the *King George V* and *Rodney*. With luck he might slow her up for them with his torpedoes.

That also was the all-important mission of the *Ark Royal*. Since noon of May 26, her shadowing planes had been hovering over the *Bismarck*. It was now time to attack her with aerial torpedoes launched from the carrier's Swordfish.

By 2:30 P.M. every aircraft available—fifteen in all—was up on the flight deck. Torpedoes were loaded and engines started. The storm still blew and the waves were high. The whole deck was drenched with spray and as slippery as a skating rink. At 2:50 the take-off began. A British observer described the scene.

> The fifteen Swordfish ranged on the pitching flight deck, each wing-tip within inches of the next... Their engines roaring... The spray from the waves dashing against their wings and soaking them ... Sailors at the chocks [which held the wheels] bracing their bodies against the driving wind and the pitch of the ship ... The Commander on the bridge trying to time his moment for the lifting of the ship, then lifting his green flag for a take-off... One plane trying to get up flying speed uphill when the ship lifted ... The next being forced to run downhill almost into the waves when the bow sank ...

It seemed a miracle to the ship's crew when all fifteen planes got off safely. The pilots had been told that they would find the *Bismarck* about forty miles to the south. Since she would be all alone, there could be no mistaking her.

Aboard the *King George V* Admiral Tovey received a radio message from Vice-Admiral Somerville advising that the Swordfish had taken off at 3:00 P.M. for a torpedo attack on the *Bismarck*. This was welcome news to the commander in chief. He knew that everything depended on the success of the planes in slowing up the enemy.

Shortly after three o'clock he was further heartened by the appearance of the *Rodney* on the horizon off the *King George V*'s port beam. By 6:00 P.M. they joined up. The older ship could make only twenty-two knots in the heavy seas and she signaled this to Tovey, who had the speed of his flagship reduced accordingly. But after a few minutes the *Rodney* signaled: "I am afraid your twenty-two knots is a bit faster than ours." Tovey remarked with a chuckle that one could almost hear the old *Rodney* panting for breath as she tried to keep up. His ship reduced speed slightly.

At such a slow pace, Sir John was reducing his chances of overtaking the *Bismarck*. In fact, he now realized he had no chance at all—unless the *Ark Royal*'s Swordfish pressed home their torpedo attack and scored enough hits to bring down the *Bismarck*'s speed by half. No planes had ever succeeded in doing that, he knew, to a battleship.

It was natural, then, that Admiral Tovey should be impatient for news from the *Ark Royal* as the crucial afternoon waned. The Swordfish should have reached their target, he calculated, by 3:30 P.M. But 4:00 P.M. came and 5:00 P.M. and 6:00 P.M.—and there was no news. The silence became almost unbearable.

It was broken at 6:30 P.M. by shattering news. Sir James Somerville radioed that his planes had failed to score any hits. Sir James did not say why. Admiral Tovey concluded that they must have been held off by the powerful anti-aircraft guns of the German battleship or handicapped by poor visibility in the storm or both. But these were not the reasons at all.

Another terrible but human error had occurred in the high-seas drama.

Because the weather was so foul and getting worse, Vice-Admiral Somerville had begun to worry that his shadowing aircraft might lose sight of the *Bismarck*. He had therefore decided to send on his cruiser *Sheffield* to establish surface contact with the enemy. She could not only shadow the *Bismarck* but also direct his planes to the exact target. So at 1:30 P.M. the *Sheffield* left Force H and made at high speed toward the German battleship.

Watchers on the *Ark Royal*, busy landing their scouting planes and preparing for the big take-off at 2:50 P.M., did not notice the cruiser slipping away. Somerville radioed the carrier of this action, and the coded message was received. But it was not immediately deciphered. The cipher staff on the *Ark Royal* was too busy at the moment decoding a stream of radio messages from the carrier's own planes shadowing the *Bismarck*.

In the meantime the Swordfish, flying blind through cloud and mist, had spotted a ship on their radar in the approximate position of the *Bismarck*. Since they had been told that the German battleship would be alone and that no British vessels were in the immediate vicinity, they dived to the attack. Roaring down out of the clouds, they clearly sighted their target and closed in. Perhaps they should have recognized that it was the *Sheffield*. For months they had been making dummy attacks on her during training in the Mediterranean. But in the heat of impending battle and in the bad visibility they did not recognize her. They began skimming over the waves toward her to launch their torpedoes.

At that precise moment, back on the *Ark Royal*, a signal officer was racing as fast as his legs would carry him on a lurching ship to the cabin of Captain Maund. The message from the Vice-Admiral about the *Sheffield* had just been decoded.

The Captain hurriedly read it. There was not a moment to lose. Desperate, dangerous measures were called for. No matter if Admiral Luetjens on the *Bismarck* heard his signals! Captain Maund immediately cast caution to the winds. He sent out an open urgent radio message in clear, uncoded English to his fliers: "WATCH OUT FOR THE SHEFFIELD! WATCH OUT FOR THE SHEFFIELD!"

It was too late.

Swordfish torpedo planes of the type from the carriers *Victorious* and *Ark Royal*

Torpedoes from the Swordfish were already churning through the water toward the *Sheffield*. Captain Larcom on the cruiser had received the signal that the Swordfish had flown off the carrier at 3:00 P.M. He was therefore expecting to see them as they flew over. He had not quite got within sight of the *Bismarck*, but he knew she was just over the horizon. He could direct the planes right on to the nearby target.

But to his amazement the British planes, when he got first sight of them, were diving straight down at him. Giving the command for full speed and a zigzag course to avoid torpedoes, he ordered his anti-aircraft guns not to fire. In this way, he was sure he would make it plain to the pilots that they were mistakenly attacking one of their own ships.

The planes, however, kept coming in and launching their torpedoes. Six or seven came dangerously close. But most of the torpedoes, Captain Larcom noticed, exploded harmlessly on hitting the water. This discovery, ironically, was to play a vital role in the drama before the long day was over.

Finally the last three planes recognized their mistake and swerved off without dropping their torpedoes.

One of them flew over the cruiser and signaled: "Sorry for the kipper!"

It was a despondent crew of pilots that brought their Swordfish back to the *Ark Royal* that afternoon. The seas were even higher than they had been when the aircraft took off. Three planes crashed on the pitching flight desk as they attempted to land. This only added to a miserable failure. Knowing that the fate of the whole enterprise depended on their crippling the *Bismarck*, the pilots had taken off full of determination. They had been told she was the only target in the vicinity. They had attacked her. But the target had turned out to be the wrong ship—one of their own.

Captain Maund had not been aware of what was happening until the plane crews returned and reported to him. He told them to forget it, that it was not really their fault. After advising them to get some hot food for their chilled bodies, he promised they would be given another chance before dark.

At 6:30 that evening Admiral Tovey heard that the *Ark Royal*'s planes had failed to hit the *Bismarck*. The report plunged him into gloom. He had no inkling that the

Swordfish had attacked the wrong ship. He assumed that they had valiantly tried to get at the German battleship but had been driven off by her flak guns or had found the visibility too bad to get in close enough for their torpedoes to take effect.

Vice-Admiral Somerville had promised a second attack before dark, but the commander in chief by this time was somewhat skeptical of carrier planes being of any use against battleships. He had had some disillusioning experiences in that regard during the last couple of days and was convinced that he could count no longer on the planes of the *Ark Royal*. Captain Vian's five destroyers would be reaching the *Bismarck* shortly before midnight. But Admiral Tovey's experience was that destroyer attacks at night seldom succeeded. He had exhausted his opportunities. He might as well face it: he had lost the race.

To complicate the situation his two battleships were running low on fuel. The oil tanks on the *King George V* were down to thirty-two per cent of capacity and those of the *Rodney* were even lower. In fact, the *Rodney* has just signaled that she would have to turn home not later than eight o'clock the next morning to refuel. The two big ships would also have to reduce speed if they hoped to get home on the oil they had. This meant that there would be increased danger from submarine and air attack.

Sir John Tovey was a realist. In addition to facing the abandonment of the chase for the *Bismarck*, galling as that was, he had to consider the risk of losing the *King George V* and the *Rodney* because of reduced speed on the way home. The *Hood* was sunk, the *Prince of Wales* crippled. His flagship was the only ship left in the British navy which could stand up to the *Bismarck* in speed and gun power. In a few months, Tovey knew, the Germans would have the *Bismarck*'s sister ship, the *Tirpitz*, ready for action. As commander in chief he could not risk so weakening the British Home Fleet as to give the Germans complete superiority in fast, heavy ships. He must preserve the *King George V* at any cost. The future demanded it.

Reluctantly and no doubt with heavy heart he radioed the Admiralty in London and Vice-Admiral Somerville on the *Renown*. He told them that unless the *Bismarck* was slowed up considerably by midnight the *King George V* would then break off the chase and return to home base to refuel. The *Rodney* would continue the pursuit until daylight.

As Sir John Tovey took his dinner in his cabin on the *King*

George V with darkness beginning to fall that evening of May 26, he could not hide his gloom. He had been after the elusive *Bismarck* for four days and nights. He had chased her for more than 2,000 miles through the stormy Atlantic. He had lost the Fleet's most powerful ship and seen one of its two newest battleships crippled and forced to return for repairs. He had come so near to his prey and then lost her. And because of a schoolboy's mistake in arithmetic, after radio-direction bearings had relocated her, he had sailed off in the wrong direction and fallen behind in the chase. Now when he was only a hundred miles from the enemy, he must abandon the pursuit because of a shortage of oil. He must admit failure and defeat.

Nor could Sir John prevent his discouragement from spreading to the crew of his flagship. It was a dark, bitter hour for all of them. They could not know that out of the gathering night and the storm, fortune at that very moment was beginning—at last—to smile on them.

CHAPTER 9

AN ELEVENTH HOUR
TURN OF FORTUNE

ABOARD THE *BISMARCK* TOWARD THE END OF A STORMY day Admiral Luetjens and his staff were waiting hopefully for the dark of night to arrive. The German Fleet Commander had known since 10:30 in the morning that he had been found again. At 11:54 he hade radioed Naval Group West: "Enemy aircraft shadowing. Land plane. Approximate position 48 40N, 20 00W." This was 600 miles from Brest, his destination.

A little later he reported that a wheeled plane was circling him. From German intelligence furnished him from shore he knew what that meant. It meant that enemy

Force H, with the battle cruiser *Renown* and the aircraft carrier *Ark Royal*, was near. The news had an ominous sound to naval headquarters in Berlin. "This marked," said the official German naval report later, "the beginning of the unfortunate developments."

Still, to those aboard the *Bismarck* it had not been a bad day. Though British carrier planes had maintained contact throughout the afternoon, none of them had launched a torpedo attack. Admiral Luetjens had expected one. But it had not come. (He had no idea that the *Ark Royal*'s Swordfish had attacked their own ship.)

It was now past 7:00 P.M. on May 26. Evening was almost upon them. Two more hours of dwindling daylight and the *Bismarck* would be safe. The planes from the enemy carrier, which were still hovering about, could not keep up their watch after dark. A British cruiser had been spotted on the horizon at 5:40 P.M. But Admiral Luetjens thought it probably could be shaken during the night.

At dawn—all would be over. The *Bismarck* would be under the cover of the mighty Luftwaffe. The Admiral had already received a radio message from Reich Marshal Hermann Goering, chief of the German air force. It said that the Reich Marshal had ordered the mobilization of every German airplane available in Western Europe. They would provide protection to the *Bismarck* on her way in to Brest. And U-boats and destroyers would help.

In another twenty-four hours or so Admiral Luetjens' daring mission would be successfully completed. Although he had not succeeded in the original aim of destroying British merchant shipping, he and his gallant crew would certainly be hailed in Germany for having sunk Britain's greatest warship, the *Hood*, with no loss to themselves. And they would be congratulated for having, after their great victory, eluded most of the ships in the British navy and got safely back to port.

In fact, according to his dispatches, Admiral Luetjens' chief worry at twilight that evening was his fuel supply. It was getting low. At 7:03 P.M. he therefore signaled home: "Fuel situation urgent. When can I expect fuel?" Probably his message was designed more to stir up Naval Group West than to get oil. For though Group West replied that it was sending out the tanker *Ermland* to refuel him during the night, the Fleet Commander knew that the ship could never get through the British, nor could he afford to stop to take on oil. He had enough fuel to make Brest at twenty knots. He merely wanted to arouse the naval command ashore.

It had been signaling him for twenty-four hours that help in the form of Luftwaffe bombers, U-boats and destroyers was on the way. None had materialized that he could see. Like most German naval officers, Admiral Luetjens resented the fact that Hitler and Goering had not given the German navy a fleet air arm such as the British had. The droning of two planes from the *Ark Royal* just out of gun range was a reminder to him of how useful carrier planes were to the enemy.

Still, though the British had known his position since before noon and their carrier could not be far away, they had done nothing about it. They had refrained from attacking all through the long afternoon. Now they had only an hour or so more of waning daylight in which to try. Perhaps the weather was too bad, the visibility too low, the waves too high, to mount an air attack from a carrier. Luck had been with the Germans insofar as the weather was concerned.

But even if the British planes did come through at the last minute, what damage could they do? The light torpedoes which the antiquated little Swordfish biplanes carried could scarcely penetrate the heavy anti-torpedo armor of the *Bismarck*. It had been built to withstand the heavier torpedoes of surface ships. Admiral Luetjens was not unduly downhearted as he stood on the bridge of the *Bismarck* toward 8:30 that evening. He was scanning

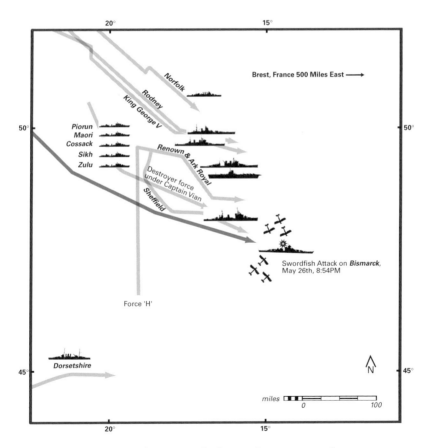

Bismarck is wounded, evening, May 26th

the eastern skies for the coming night that would preserve his ship and his victory.

And then the antiquated little enemy planes appeared.

The air-raid alarm sounded throughout the battleship. A voice blared through the loudspeakers: "All hands to action stations!" From the lookouts came cries: "Plane on the starboard bow! ... Plane on the port beam! ... Plane on the starboard quarter!"

The old-fashioned Swordfish, one of the few types of biplanes still being used in combat, were swarming in from all directions. The *Bismarck*'s guns roared into action, puncturing the sky with the bursts of their shells.

Admiral Luetjens hastily got off an urgent radio message to shore: "20:54. [8:54 P.M.] Am being attacked by carrier-borne aircraft!"

On the *Ark Royal,* as daylight started to fade, the crew was working feverishly to get off the second and final strike against the *Bismarck.* All hands knew it was the last chance.

The fiasco of the attack on the cruiser *Sheffield* had at least revealed one vital piece of information to the carrier's commander. Captain Larcom, restraining his feelings about having been nearly sunk by the *Ark Royal*'s planes, radioed over to Captain Maund that most of the torpedoes launched by the Swordfish had exploded on hitting the water. In fact, that had saved the *Sheffield* from disaster.

Captain Maund on the *Ark Royal* concluded at once that the new magnetic pistols on his aerial torpedoes would have to be discarded. He ordered them replaced by the old-fashioned contact pistols. These went off only when they hit a solid object. In the high waves, torpedoes tended to dive lower than they were set to go. They often went under a ship. Theoretically a magnetic torpedo, even when it slid under a ship, would explode because of its nearness to the steel of a vessel's hull. That was why Captain Maund had used them in the first attack. But for some reason most of them had gone off on hitting the water. He therefore decided to try the old contact kind. To guard against their diving harmlessly under the *Bismarck*, he set the torpedoes for a diving depth of only ten feet.

He made sure this time that the Swordfish would not mistake the *Sheffield* for the *Bismarck*. The pilots were told to fly over the cruiser first and then go on to the enemy ship.

The *Sheffield*, having by this time sighted the *Bismarck*, was shadowing her just out of gun range. She could therefore direct the fliers straight to their target. This was a great help, as the Germans ultimately realized. In the secret official German naval report written afterward, Admiral Kurt Assmann emphasized that "this was of particular importance for the further course of action since the *Sheffield* was now in a position to direct the torpedo aircraft in an attack on the *Bismarck*."

Actually, despite this help, the British fliers found it very difficult to locate the enemy in the murky weather. A northwest wind was blowing with almost gale force. The clouds were down to 600 feet above the churning sea. Getting the planes off the carrier for the final attack had proved most difficult. The *Ark Royal* was pitching even more dangerously than during the previous take-off. But a few minutes after 7:00 P.M. fifteen Swordfish— all that were left—got safely off the lurching flight deck and headed for contact with the *Sheffield*. They knew that everything depended on them. If they failed this time to hit and drastically slow up the *Bismarck*, she would make her haven at Brest.

The planes reached the *Sheffield* forty minutes later and were told by signal that the *Bismarck* lay twelve miles dead ahead. In eight or nine minutes the attack would be launched. Observers on the cruiser listened for the sound of firing from the *Bismarck*'s guns. Ten minutes passed, fifteen minutes, thirty minutes. The silence was ominous. What had happened to the planes?

They had got lost in the clouds. At the end of half an hour they were back over the *Sheffield* asking for a fresh bearing. The *Bismarck*, they were told, was still just twelve miles directly ahead. The planes swerved off for another try.

Soon the watchers on the cruiser heard the roar of anti-aircraft fire from the *Bismarck*. Now and then a clear patch in the mist revealed the flashes of her guns and the bursts of the shells in the air. At last the Swordfish had found their target and were attacking.

It was hard going. So thick was the cloud cover—it rose from a few hundred feet above the sea to 10,000 feet—that the British planes could not hold formation for the sweep down at the German battleship. They soon split up. To make matters worse their wings began to ice up while they were in the clouds. The only recourse was for each pilot to get down and attack as best he could. The result was that they flew in from every direction to launch their torpedoes. This had one advantage, of course. It dispersed the German fire.

Even so, the anti-aircraft fire, as the airmen soon found, was quite deadly. At least five planes were soon hit, though they managed to keep going. All but one of the fifteen Swordfish launched their torpedoes at short range in the teeth of the heavy flak barrage.

Did they score any hits? It was difficult to see in the smoke of battle and in the mist and gathering night. The last plane did not launch its torpedo until 9:25. Night was falling. Apparently there had been no hits. At least that was what the squadron leader ruefully reported by radio to his carrier, which in turn flashed the mournful news to Admiral Tovey on the *King George V*.

"Estimate no hits!" That signal from the squadron leader was the last bitter straw for the commander in chief of the Home Fleet. There was nothing for him to do now but admit failure and turn home. It would be of no use to try to catch the *Bismarck* during the night. She had too big a lead on him.

The exhausted crews who had been pushing the two big battleships *Rodney* and *King George V* in a desperate effort to overhaul the *Bismarck* were informed of the failure. Captain Dalrymple-Hamilton on the *Rodney* personally took the microphone to inform his crew over the ship's loud-speakers that no hits had been scored by the Swordfish. The chase seemed to be at an end.

The spirits of the British aboard the two ships were about as black as the night which had now descended over the wind-swept sea. Then over the radio came a message which at first merely seemed to confuse the situation. Admiral Tovey could make nothing of it.

It was a signal from the *Sheffield* announcing that the *Bismarck* had reversed course. Instead of steering southeast for Brest she was now veering in the opposite direction! To the dispirited Sir John it made no sense. He knew that sailors often made the mistake of making out the course of a distant ship 180 degrees wrong. That is, they thought it was coming toward them when it actually was steaming away from them. Sir John, who invariably kept his temper tightly in check, permitted himself a sarcastic remark at the *Sheffield*'s making such a common blunder. And at this, of all moments!

But Captain Larcom on the *Sheffield* had deadly proof that he was right. If he had mentioned it in his message the Admiral would have been convinced, but the Captain had neglected to do so. The proof was that shortly before the

Swordfish had finished their attack on the *Bismarck*, the German battleship had turned suddenly on the British ship and opened fire. Before the *Sheffield* could make smoke and swerve off, one salvo from the enemy ship had fallen so close that the splinters wounded twelve men among the cruiser's anti-aircraft crews. Three of them were dying.

The *Bismarck* had not, as Captain Larcom expected, turned back on its course to Brest after firing. Instead it continued to come at him on the opposite course, and he had to scurry to get out of range and save his ship from being blown up by the enemy's heavy guns. It was clear to Captain Larcom that the *Bismarck* was in fact sailing directly toward Sir John's two battleships to the north.

But this, at first, was not clear to the Admiral. He had just dismissed the *Sheffield*'s report with a sarcastic quip when a second message came over the radio about the *Bismarck*'s new course. This was from one of the planes of the *Ark Royal* which had remained over the German battleship to see whether any damage had been done in the second torpedo attack. The pilot could not see any damage but he could see plainly that the *Bismarck* was heading northwest.

Sir John's face lit up. A ship's watch at nearly sea level could mistake the direction of a ship directly ahead.

But a plane just above could not. The pilot's confirmation of the *Sheffield*'s signal was significant. Still, Sir John refused to be carried away by this good news. If the *Bismarck* were really, for unaccountable reasons, steering toward him, he would have her before dawn. But he thought the chances were that she had merely reversed course as part of an evasive action against the Swordfish attack. Or she could have done so in order to catch the *Sheffield* unawares and finish her off. Then, with the night ahead of him, Admiral Luetjens would shake his shadowers and have clear sailing until daylight brought him his shore-based bomber cover.

If Tovey had known of the *Bismarck*'s firing at the *Sheffield*, this would only have confirmed his judgment. As it was, he was sure that the next message would reveal that the enemy had resumed course for Brest.

To Sir John's surprise—and it was a pleasant surprise— the next message did not reveal any such thing. It came nine minutes later from a spotter plane. It said the *Bismarck* was still steering northwest. Again, after nine more minutes, a similar report was received from the aircraft. And then came a second dispatch from the *Sheffield*. The *Bismarck*, it said, had now veered north.

Admiral Tovey's skepticism began to evaporate. It was obvious now that the *Bismarck* was steering toward him. It made no sense. . . . What could the explanation be? Suddenly it occurred to the Admiral that the *Ark Royal's* planes might have scored a hit after all. If so, it must have been just the lucky one he needed. It must have damaged the *Bismarck's* rudders. That would explain her erring course. As soon as he had read the *Sheffield's* last intelligence, Admiral Tovey changed course to the south to meet the enemy head on.

Shortly after dusk the *Sheffield*, following the *Bismarck* north at a respectable distance, sighted five destroyers tossing at high speed through the rough seas. They turned out to be Captain Vian's squadron. Captain Larcom directed them on to the enemy ship just ahead.

The last of the little Swordfish torpedo planes did not get back to the *Ark Royal* until after dark. Five of them were riddled with shrapnel from the *Bismarck's* flak. One had 175 holes in it. Both the pilot and his gunner were wounded, but they had succeeded in bringing back their crippled craft. They managed to land it on the flight deck, though the ship still pitched and rolled in the storm.

The pilots reported to Captain Maund that they were sure they had scored at least one torpedo hit amidships. This information was radioed to the fleet at 10:30 P.M. Ten minutes later the carrier signaled that the pilots believed they had made a second hit on the *Bismarck*'s starboard quarter. For some reason Admiral Tovey did not receive this message until an hour later. He had already turned south. But the message confirmed him in his judgment. Any damage to a ship's quarter might put her rudder and even her propellers out of action. He was now pretty certain that this was what had happened to the *Bismarck*.

Toward midnight he radioed the rest of the fleet and the Admiralty in London of his new course on the enemy. His plan now was to get to the westward of the *Bismarck* and attack her at dawn when she would be silhouetted against the light of daybreak. So confident was Admiral Tovey now—after a week of reverses—that he penned a message to the officers and crew of his flagship.

> The sinking of the *Bismarck* may have an effect on the war as a whole out of all proportion to the loss to the enemy of one battleship.
> May God be with you and grant you victory.

· · ·

About one o'clock in the morning—it was now May 27—
Sir John received a message from Vice-Admiral Somerville
that further increased his confidence. The last of the *Ark
Royal's* planes assigned to keep contact with the *Bismarck*
had returned during the night with a vital piece of information. Its pilot had seen her turn two complete circles after the torpedo attack and come to a virtual stop headed
north against the wind.

For the British this was the final piece in the jigsaw
puzzle. The mighty *Bismarck* had been hit in the stern. Her
rudders or propellers—or both—had been damaged. She
was no longer maneuverable.

The chase which had seemed definitely lost a few hours
before had been nearly won. This was a sudden last-
minute turn of fortune! Admiral Tovey could now take on
the *Bismarck* at any hour he chose. It was a temptation for
him to close in at once and try to dispose of the enemy during the night. But now, he saw, was the moment to keep
cool. There were so many British warships converging on
the scene that there was danger of their firing on each other in the rainswept darkness. He would wait until dawn.
In the meantime Captain Vian's destroyers, which had
reported sighting the *Bismarck* two hours earlier, could

keep him informed throughout the rest of the night of the enemy's exact position.

As a matter of fact, the dashing destroyer leader had already gone into action on his own initiative.

CHAPTER 10

A DESPERATE NIGHT
ON THE *BISMARCK*

IN THE VERY LAST HOUR OF DAYLIGHT ON MAY 26, WHEN the squadron of Swordfish came in to attack the *Bismarck*, the German battleship had swung into action as quickly and efficiently as when she had sunk the *Hood* and held off the torpedo planes of the *Victorious* two days before.

Most of the 2,400 officers and men aboard were dead tired from lack of sleep. For nearly a week the gunnery crews had remained at their guns, snatching what little sleep they could. It was not much.

The strict admiral had insisted on these precautions. Luetjens never knew at what second an enemy warship or plane might loom out of the clouds or mist. He had to be ready for instant action. The swarm of Swordfish suddenly swooping down out of the clouds had shown how necessary it was.

The German sailors felt certain that this would be the last bit of action on the voyage. That afternoon Admiral Luetjens had assured them over the loudspeakers that by dawn of the next day they would be safely under the cover of the Luftwaffe. Within twenty-four hours they would be comfortably ashore. The sailors, though weary, were in a fairly cocky mood. What could a handful of out-of-date British carrier planes do to their mighty battleship? Shooting them down would be good target practice.

Confidently, Admiral Luetjens watched the ship's brand-new flak guns fire away at the darting dots of the approaching aircraft. He was a little tense and tight-lipped, as he always was in battle. But he did not appear to the others on the bridge to be much worried.

Two evenings before, in a similarly fading light east of Greenland, the *Bismarck* had easily beaten off an attack of the same kind of torpedo-carrying biplanes. Those had come off the *Victorious*. One of the aircraft had scored a hit on the starboard side, but it had not slowed up the *Bismarck* by one single knot.

There was little chance, Admiral Luetjens thought, that this new Swordfish attack—the very last one he would have to face before reaching Brest—would be any more successful. Carrier planes, he remarked to Captain Lindemann, had never seriously damaged a battleship in history. They were like a swarm of bees. They could sting but not injure you. For one thing their torpedoes were too light.

Nevertheless, he did not intend to risk being hit again by any of them. He directed Captain Lindemann to zigzag to avoid torpedoes and to employ some of his smaller guns in exploding them should any come near. This soon became necessary. The torpedoes came skimming through the water from all points of the compass. Most of them were exploded harmlessly some distance away by gunfire.

Two were not. In a split second one of these changed the whole course of this nearly week-old drama at sea and brought it swiftly to a climax.

Curiously enough, that one fatal British aerial torpedo might not have been launched at all if a certain German

U-boat, an hour earlier, had not found itself in the strangest position imaginable.

This was the U-566, commanded by Lieutenant Wohlfarth. It was returning from a long operation at sea when, on the late afternoon of May 26, a lookout reported sighting enemy warships. The submarine crash-dived. When it edged up again toward the surface, Lieutenant Wohlfarth saw through his periscope that he had come up right between the battle cruiser *Renown* and the carrier *Ark Royal*. The battle cruiser was just ahead of him. The carrier was just behind. In fact the U-boat commander could see, he later reported, the planes of the *Ark Royal*'s deck warming up for a take-off.

All he had to do to prevent that take-off was to launch torpedoes from his stern. At the same moment he could fire torpedoes at the *Renown* from his bow. He was so near both ships he couldn't miss. It was one of those positions a submarine skipper dreams of having but rarely, if ever, has. Here were two big enemy ships in line with each other, and he was directly between them. It was not even necessary to aim his torpedo tubes, because the bow and the stern of his ship were pointed directly at the two big targets.

There was another, more important reason why it was not necessary to aim them, as Lieutenant Wohlfarth bitterly realized. His torpedo tubes were empty! He had fired every single one of his torpedoes at British merchant ships during his previous operation.

Completely frustrated, the U-boat commander watched in his periscope the two great sitting ducks speed out of range. He saw the Swordfish take off from the carrier and sweep away toward the *Bismarck*. If only he had had a torpedo or two, they would never have got off that flight deck! There would have been no deck left. And the mighty *Bismarck*—though Lieutenant Wohlfarth, of course, didn't know this at the time—might have been saved.

As soon as the *Renown* and the *Ark Royal* were out of gun range, Lieutenant Wohlfarth surfaced, strung up his wireless sender, and got off a message to Brest. It was among the secret German naval papers obtained after the war.

> 20:00. [8:00 P.M.] One battleship, one aircraft carrier in approximate position 47 50 North, 16 50 West. Course 115 degrees. High speed.

The *Bismarck* took in the signal. At that hour she had not

yet seen any of the carrier planes. But it was helpful to Admiral Luetjens to know from the U-boat just where Force H was and in which direction and at what speed it was proceeding. He did not understand why the carrier had not sent over attacking planes. But for an hour or so— until dark—he must be on the lookout for them.

At 8:54 P.M. he had reported that they had come and were attacking. For several hectic minutes he had watched them gallantly cut through his flak fire and come in to launch their torpedoes. But the torpedoes that had not been destroyed by his own gunfire had passed wide of his ship.

Apparently no one on the *Bismarck* saw one British plane steal in from behind. But lookouts aft quickly reported a torpedo thrashing toward the stern. The target at that angle is very small—only the width of a ship at its narrow end. It seemed certain that the torpedo was sure to miss.

Then it hit. There was an explosion. The stern of the *Bismarck* shuddered. Later, one surviving gunner remembered hearing a desperate voice shouting through the intercom: "Rudder jamming hard to starboard! Ship circling!"

Admiral Luetjens was on the bridge with Captain Lindemann, taking in the shattering reports. As soon as the ship veered and started to circle he understood what had happened.

"Get divers down to clear the rudders!" he snapped.

A message came up from the steering engine room. It had been knocked out.

"Couple the hand-steering!" the Captain barked. Damage-control parties went quickly to work. Two divers went overboard to try to clear the jammed rudders. To keep up the morale of the crew, false news was broadcast on the ship's loud-speakers. A seaman later remembered it. One broadcast said the hand-steering had been coupled on. A second, thirty minutes later, announced that the rudders had been cleared.

Admiral Luetjens knew better. He was a man of few illusions. At 9:05 P.M., eleven minutes after he radioed Group West that he was being attacked by carrier planes, he got off an urgent message: "21:05. Ship no longer maneuverable!"

Within the minute he rushed off another: "21:05. Approximate position 47 40 North, 14 50 West. Torpedo hit aft."

Ten minutes later he sent a third message: "21:15. Torpedo hit midships."

After the British planes, as soon as darkness fell, came the British destroyers.

At 11:25 that evening Admiral Luetjens sent out a signal to shore: "Am surrounded by *Renown* and light forces."

Those "light forces" now attacked in the pitch darkness of the stormy night. They were Captain Vian's five destroyers. They had sighted the *Bismarck* at 10:38 P.M. and a few minutes later the battleship had opened fire on them with her big guns. Captain Vian's chief job was to shadow the *Bismarck* during the night—as added insurance to the trailing by the cruiser *Sheffield*. Then in the morning the battleships *King George V* and *Rodney* would finish her off.

But Captain Vian was a dashing, intrepid officer. He could not stay out of a fight if there was any chance of getting into one. At great risk to his small ships from the heavy guns of the enemy, he closed in to launch torpedoes. The *Bismarck* was already unmaneuverable. Nothing that the destroyers could do would make her any more so. One cannot escape the conclusion that Captain Vian wished to sink her himself. After all, the battleships and cruisers had had their chance and—up to now—had failed. So he charged in with his little destroyers.

Each of them was nearly destroyed by the accurate fire from the German battleship. Her gunners were making good use of her radar in the darkness. The very first salvo against Captain Vian's own *Cossack* destroyed part of her radio antenna. Splinters from the shells of another salvo wounded three men on the *Zulu*. The other three destroyers, *Maori*, *Sikh* and *Piorun* (the last being a Polish ship), worked around the *Bismarck* so as to disperse her fire. But the battleship's guns were aiming well. The destroyers could not get close enough to aim their torpedoes effectively. Still, all night they kept charging in until they had shot their last torpedo.

None of them scored a hit. And indeed Captain Vian was later criticized in some naval circles for needlessly risking his ships. As it was, the destroyers, dodging and twisting about in the battle, lost contact with the *Bismarck* several times during the night, thus risking failure in their main job.

At 2:30 in the morning Admiral Tovey signaled them to fire star shells to indicate the *Bismarck*'s position to him. He was getting close but was not yet in sight. The destroyers fired some star shells, drawing heavy fire from the German battleships as a result. Yet at 3:00 A.M. Captain Vian lost his prey and did not regain contact until almost dawn. Admiral Tovey, who had lost the *Bismarck* so many times during the week, was understandably worried.

Undoubtedly this night attack in foul weather by the British destroyers was foolhardy. But despite its failure to obtain a single torpedo hit, it did serve one purpose. It kept the German gun crews so busy all night that they were completely exhausted by morning.

And it helped to remind Admiral Luetjens that his end was near. Behind the destroyers, he knew, were British battleships and cruisers. His radio-detection officers had been picking up their signals all night. The *Bismarck*'s guns were firing well. They were showing their accuracy against the darting destroyers. But with his ship's rudders jammed, Admiral Luetjens knew that he could not hold his own with the enemy battleships, as he had against the *Hood* and the *Prince of Wales* in the first battle.

The *Bismarck* was doomed and the Admiral knew it.

At 11:40 P.M., while the ship was still floundering along helplessly but nevertheless keeping up a continuous fire on the British destroyers, he got off a radio message to the Fatherland.

> Ship no longer maneuverable. We fight to the last shell. Long live the Führer!

Eighteen minutes later he broke the news directly to the Führer, Adolf Hitler, dictator of Germany. He radioed:

> 23:58. To the Führer of the German Reich, Adolf Hitler. We fight to the last in our belief in you, my Führer, and in the firm faith in Germany's victory!

A minute later he sent out a general signal.

> 23:59. Armament and engines still intact. Ship however cannot be steered.

With the end almost certain as soon as daylight broke, Admiral Luetjens gave thought to how he could get the *Bismarck*'s log safely home. It seemed important that the Naval Command and Hitler himself should understand his strategy and tactics and how fate had turned against him at the very end.

Three of the ship's five Arado 196 scouting planes were

still undamaged. The Admiral ordered them launched. One was to carry the *Bismarck*'s log. All three would take home letters from the officers and crew—the very last letters to families and sweethearts, perhaps, that the young men would ever write. The airmen were the envy of the sailors. They at least would get out alive.

Letters were hastily written as best they could be in the midst of the battle with the British destroyers. It would be difficult to launch the planes in the high seas, stiff wind and darkness. But the pilots were confident they could take off. The ship's log and several mail pouches were loaded into the three planes. The first one was hoisted on the ship's catapult. Its engine was started. The pilot waved farewell.

He never got off. Somehow the torpedo which struck aft had damaged the compressed-air feed to the catapult. Desperate efforts were made to repair it. They proved unsuccessful. In despair the pilots finally climbed down from their cockpits. Their mail would never be delivered to the loved ones at home—at least, not by air. The ship's log would have to remain aboard.

This was a further despairing moment for the men on the *Bismarck*. Most of them were still working themselves to a point of exhaustion at the guns, which continued to bang away at the enemy destroyers.

Then, as so often happens at sea during the desperate hours, rumors began to fly through the ship. The first German submarine had arrived in the vicinity. More were just behind. Eighty-one Luftwaffe bombers were on the way out. They and the U-boats would make short shrift of the British tormentors. Two big tugboats had put out from Brest. They would haul the *Bismarck* safely into port.

Many a sailor started to sing, but not for long. Radio messages from the homeland in response to Admiral Luetjen's desperate dispatches were beginning to arrive. Captain Lindemann read them over the loud-speakers to the crews. He must have thought they would cheer up the hard-pressed men. They had, however, the opposite effect. They seemed to confirm the hopeless plight of the great battleship.

Seven minutes before two o'clock in the morning, two messages came over the radio from Adolf Hitler himself.

01:53. To Fleet Commander:
      I thank you in the name of the German people.
                              Adolf Hitler

To the crew of the battleship *Bismarck*:
The whole of Germany is with you. What can
still be done will be done. The performance of
your duty will strengthen our people in the
struggle for their existence.   Adolf Hitler

Such words sounded ominous to the crew. Grimly they fought on at their guns. Shortly after two o'clock there was a pause in the firing. Admiral Luetjens thought of his chief artillery officer who had done such a magnificent job in sinking the *Hood*. At 2:21 A.M. he radioed Grand Admiral Erich Raeder in Berlin about him.

02:21. To Commander in Chief of the Navy:
Propose Lieutenant Commander Schneider,
gunnery officer, be awarded Knights Cross
for sinking *Hood*.   Fleet Commander.

Within an hour and a half, there was a reply.

03:51. Berlin. To Lieutenant Commander Schneider:
The Führer has awarded you the Knights Cross
for sinking the battle cruiser, *Hood*. Heartiest
congratulations.
                    Commander in Chief of the Navy.

On the swaying bridge of the Bismarck, drenched by spray from the wind and the waves, there was a touching little ceremony just as the ship's bells sounded 4:00 A.M.

Admiral Luetjens read the radiograph to Lieutenant Commander Schneider and congratulated him. The cold and taciturn admiral was almost in tears. So was his brilliant gunnery officer.

After 3:00 A.M. the British destroyers appeared to have given up their futile attack. A lull set in—the lull before the storm. Both sides were waiting for the dawn—the British joyfully, the Germans with despair. Aboard the crippled *Bismarck* there were few illusions about what daylight would bring.

The destroyers reappeared toward 6:00 A.M., in the closing moments of darkness, and the German battleship opened fire on the nearest one. This was the *Maori*, which approached to within 9,000 yards and fired her last two torpedoes. She then ducked away from the *Bismarck*'s 15-inch shells. There were no hits by either side.

At 6:25 on the morning of May 27, Admiral Luetjens radioed Naval Group West that the situation remained unchanged. At 7:10, in the first dim rays of daylight, he dispatched another signal: "Send U-boat to save War Diary [log]."

It was the last message he ever sent.

CHAPTER 11

FINAL BATTLE: THE SINKING OF THE *BISMARCK*

TO THE MEN ON THE BATTLESHIPS *KING GEORGE V* AND the *Rodney*, waiting impatiently for the kill, it seemed, as one officer later wrote, that the dawn would never come.

The crews were at their battle stations all through the long night, though half of them at a time were given permission to snatch some sleep at their posts. The captains of the two ships remained at their compass platforms. They kept track of the plotting of their own positions and that of the enemy, as reported during the night by the destroyers which were snapping at the heels of the *Bismarck*.

They also kept scanning the eastern sky for the first faint hint of dawn. When Commander W. J. C. Robertson, chief of staff for operations, thought he saw it, he went down to his cabin on the *King George V* to fetch his steel helmet. He was amused to see four large rats scurrying about in terror. Apparently even the rats aboard knew the ship was going into battle.

The commander in chief also had been up most of the night, taking in the signals from the destroyers and waiting as impatiently as everyone else for the daylight to break. Admiral Tovey still didn't know exactly where his prey was. For nearly a week the thick clouds had hidden the sun by day and the stars by night. The ships could not get a bearing. They had to plot their position as well as that of the *Bismarck* by dead reckoning. This was never completely accurate.

For this reason the commander in chief during the night had asked Captain Vian's destroyers to fire star shells to indicate the *Bismarck*'s location. But in the rain and low clouds he had not been able to see them over the horizon.

It soon became obvious that daylight was not going to bring any improvement in the weather. As the skies began gradually to lighten on May 27, the clouds still hung close to the sea. The rain did not let up. The seas remained high. The wind blew out of the northwest as strong as ever. In the wretched visibility Sir John began to search for the *Bismarck*. Because of the fuel shortage of both his battleships, he knew he had to find the German leviathan and sink her within two or three hours at the most. By 10:00 A.M. they would have just enough oil to limp home.

At this critical juncture the cruiser *Norfolk* came to his aid, as she had at the beginning of the chase off Iceland. Though herself dangerously low on oil, she had been racing south all night to get in on the fight. At 8:15 A.M. her lookouts sighted the *Bismarck* eight miles dead ahead. Captain Phillips turned his cruiser hard over to get quickly out of range of the big ship's guns. As he swerved he sighted the *Rodney* and *King George V* in the distance. He could thus serve as a visual link between them and the enemy.

Admiral Tovey's two ships were actually off course. Had it not been for the *Norfolk* the commander in chief might have missed the *Bismarck* once again. Quickly he altered course. Twenty-eight minutes later he finally sighted his target twelve miles directly ahead. It was the first time he had actually seen the *Bismarck*. After nearly a week of frustrating, nerve-wracking pursuit, he had cornered her at last.

He moved in at once for the kill. He could see that the *Bismarck* was moving very slowly, headed into the wind. But he had no reason to doubt that Admiral Luetjens could still use his excellent guns with customary accuracy. The German battleship had managed to dispose of the *Hood* in a few minutes.

Admiral Tovey signaled to the *Rodney*, which was about a mile off to his port side. He told her she was free to move and to fire as she thought best but should conform generally to the flagship's maneuvers. He was not going to fight the rigid battle that had cost the fleet the *Hood*.

At precisely 8:47 A.M. on May 27 the *Rodney* opened fire with her 16-inch guns. Within the minute the *King George V* got off her first salvo of 14-inch shells. The *Bismarck* did not reply for about two minutes. But when she did, her fire was accurate. Her third salvo straddled the *Rodney*, on which she concentrated her big guns, and almost scored a direct hit.

Captain Dalrymple-Hamilton on the *Rodney* turned a little to port so he could bring all his guns into action. Soon he was pounding the *Bismarck* with full broadsides.

The *King George V* plowed straight ahead. In this position she was unable to use her aft guns. But she was rapidly closing the range. The cruiser *Norfolk*, which had refrained from firing at the *Bismarck* during the earlier action with the *Hood* and the *Prince of Wales*, now joined in the battle. She began firing with her 8-inch guns at 20,000 yards.

A second British cruiser soon entered the fray. This was the *Dorsetshire*. She had been escorting a convoy 600 miles west of Cape Finisterre on the morning of May 26 when she picked up the signal that the *Bismarck* had been found again. Captain B. C. S. Martin saw that the enemy was a mere 300 miles almost due north of him. On his own he left the convoy and steamed off at twenty-eight knots to try to get in on some action. He had arrived on the scene just in time. At 9:04 A.M. the *Dorsetshire* turned her 8-inch guns on the enemy and opened fire.

Thus by shortly after nine o'clock the *Bismarck*, helpless to take avoiding action because of the damage to her rudders, was being shelled by two British battleships and two heavy cruisers. Such superiority soon began to tell. The British warships were now scoring direct hits with their big shells. One of the first salvos was seen to knock away part of the *Bismarck*'s bridge. The German guns, though still blazing away, were losing accuracy.

At one minute before nine o'clock, Sir John turned his flagship south so he could bring a full broadside against the enemy. The *Rodney* followed her. They were both now only 15,000 yards from the German ship, which was yawing roughly north. After fifteen minutes of continuous exchange of salvos Admiral Tovey found that he had passed the *Bismarck*. He turned his ships around for another run parallel to the enemy, this time northward.

The range had lowered to a bare 8,000 yards. Both the *Rodney* and *King George V* were delivering full broadsides as fast as their big guns could be reloaded. The *Bismarck* was obviously hurt from such a murderous fire at such close range. A large fire was seen belching smoke and flame amidships. Some of her 15-inch guns were no longer firing. A lookout on the *Norfolk* saw two of them drop almost to the water line. Others pointed crazily at the sky. Their hydraulic controls, it was evident, were no longer functioning. One gun turret was blown clear away, its twisted metal toppling against the bridge.

About ten o'clock, a little more than an hour after the action had started, the last of the *Bismarck*'s guns were silenced. She had been reduced to a flaming, smoking, battered hulk. Through the jagged shell holes in her side could be seen the bright flames of fires consuming her insides.

And yet above the blazing inferno the *Bismarck's* flag still flew. She was beaten. She was finished. But she would not surrender.

It is almost impossible to reconstruct the holocaust as it was experienced at his hour by the 2,400 Germans aboard the battered battleship. Each of the 118 survivors later had a tale of horror to tell. But only three of them were officers, all of junior rank. The overall picture as seen from the bridge can never be told. Admiral Luetjens did not send out a single message about this last battle. He did not even signal, as was customary, that it had begun.

He could not, in any case, have sent many messages. One of the first salvos from the British battleships blew away the admiral's bridge and with it Admiral Guenther Luetjens. Captain Lindemann might have survived. Miraculously he escaped injury even when his bridge was demolished by a British shell. Junior officers urged him to jump overboard with them when it became clear that the ship was doomed. But he stuck to his post to the end.

Battered and silent and afire though she was, the *Bismarck* would neither surrender nor sink!

Admiral Tovey thought his guns had poured enough heavy shells into her to sink a dozen battleships. During the run to the south the *Rodney* had fired six torpedoes at the *Bismarck* and the *Norfolk* had fired four in an effort to dispatch her by this means. All had missed. But the bombardment by both heavy and light guns had not let up for a moment. And still the flaming enemy hulk kept afloat.

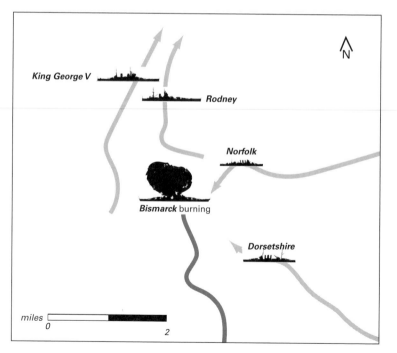

Bismarck is sunk, May 27th

The commander in chief was both puzzled and impatient. He had never imagined that a ship could take so much punishment and not go down. Time was getting short. German long-range bombers from France had been reported approaching. German U-boats were known to be converging on the scene. The *Rodney* and *King George V* were already zigzagging as they fired. This was a necessary precaution against hostile submarines. Worst of all, the oil tanks on the two British battleships were so low by ten o'clock that Tovey was not sure he would have enough fuel to get them home.

Impatiently the Admiral sent orders to Captain Patterson on the bridge of the *King George V*.

"Get closer! Get in there closer! I can't see enough hits!"

The two battleships plowed in closer, the *Rodney* turning so she could fire with all her nine 16-inch guns. She also dispatched her last two torpedoes at a range of only 3,000 yards. One of them hit—the first occasion in naval history that a battleship had ever torpedoed another. The *Norfolk* also launched her last four torpedoes at 4,000 yards. One of them hit, but still the *Bismarck* did not go down.

Vice-Admiral Somerville asked for another try at it

with his Swordfish from the *Ark Royal*. They had disabled the *Bismarck* in the first place. Perhaps they could finish the job!

The planes took off from the carrier at 9:25 A.M., but as soon as they arrived over the German battleship they saw that it would be impossible to get down to launch their torpedoes. The shell fire from their own ships was too intense. The squadron leader signaled Admiral Tovey asking that he cease fire while the planes made their run to the target.

There was no reply—except from the *King George V*'s anti-aircraft guns, which started to fire at the Swordfish in the belief they were German planes. Captain Patterson noticed the mistake at once and told the officer commanding the flak guns to desist.

"Can't you see our airmen waving at you?" he asked.

"I thought they were Huns shaking their fists at us," the officer replied.

It was now 10:15 A.M., and Admiral Tovey had to make a hard decision. It was absolutely imperative for him to turn his big ships home. On their dwindling oil reserves, they could make only a slow speed as it was. This would add to their peril if the German bombers and submarines attacked.

He looked over a last time at the burning wreck of the ship he had been firing at with all the guns and torpedo tubes of the fleet. She still floated. But he knew she was finished. She would never make port. Satisfied that he had destroyed her but disappointed at not having sunk her, he ordered the *Rodney* to form behind him as he set course northeast for Britain.

As he steered for home he sent back one last signal. If any of the cruisers or destroyers had any more torpedoes they might launch them point-blank in a final effort to send the battered *Bismarck* to the bottom.

The cruiser *Dorsetshire*, which had arrived just in time to see some action, had three torpedoes left. Her skipper, Captain Martin, had not waited for the Admiral's last order. When he saw the two big battleships turn for home he acted on his own. He closed in to within 3,500 yards. Two of his torpedoes were sent skimming toward the *Bismarck*'s starboard side. One of them hit just under the remains of her bridge, toppling what was left of it. The time was 10:20 A.M.

Then he circled to the port side and at 10:36 fired his last torpedo at 2,500 yards. It tore a big hole at the water line. Slowly the *Bismarck*, her flag still flying, heeled over to the port side and turned upside-down. Then she sank beneath the waves. The clock on the *Dorsetshire* bridge read 10:40 A.M.

At that moment Captain Martin took in the Admiral's signal to try to sink the *Bismarck* with his remaining torpedoes. He replied that he had just done so and that the *Bismarck* had gone down.

The great British fleet quickly dispersed. The *Ark Royal's* Swordfish, still in the air, jettisoned their torpedoes. It was too dangerous to land with them on the carrier's deck. When they returned they found the *Ark Royal* under attack by German bombers that had finally reached the scene. Vice-Admiral Somerville, as soon as the Swordfish had safely landed, ordered Force H to head full steam south toward its base at Gibraltar. Despite the arrival of German bombers and the reported presence of U-boats near by, the British navy still had an errand of mercy to perform. The murderous bombardment of the *Bismarck* had not killed all the members of her crew. Miraculously, several hundred men had survived the blazing inferno, though many of these were wounded. They could now be seen from the British ships, clinging to debris in the water or swimming about in great patches of oil.

The cruiser *Dorsetshire* and the destroyer *Maori* moved quickly in to rescue them. It was impossible in the high seas to lower boats to pick them up. But life lines were thrown out and jumping ladders strung over the sides of the two ships. Most of the German sailors were too badly wounded or too exhausted to hoist themselves up the lines or ladders. The British crews went to work to haul them up. One officer on the *Dorsetshire*, a Lieutenant Carver, jumped overboard to save some of those who were drowning or choking to death from having swallowed oil.

On the decks of the two rescue ships first aid was given to the German survivors as soon as they were hauled up. Oxygen was administered, stomachs pumped out, oil washed off. Injections of morphine were given to relieve pain.

And then occurred the last irony of the great sea drama. A lookout on the *Dorsetshire* cried out: "Periscope on the starboard bow!" A general alarm sounded: "All hands to action stations!" Reluctantly and with heavy heart, Captain Martin had to give the order to abandon the rescue operation and make away, zigzagging, to avoid the torpedoes of the German submarine.

Rescue of *Bismarck* survivors by HMS *Dorsetshire*

And final irony of all: the German U-boat whose periscope appeared—it was the U-74—had no torpedoes left! But the British could not know this. The *Dorsetshire*, with eighty-three survivors aboard, and the *Maori*, with thirty, steamed off to get away from the torpedoless U-boat. Several hundred German sailors, whom the two ships could have saved had not the German submarine appeared, were left to drown in the cold stormy sea. The U-74 took some time to surface. She was able to pick up only three men alive. A German steamer, the *Sachsenwald*, rescued two more. Of the 2,400 men on the *Bismarck*, only 118 survived.

Thus the chase ended. It had taken the British navy a week to bring it to a successful conclusion. It had taken eight battleships and battle cruisers, two aircraft carriers, four heavy cruisers, seven light cruisers, twenty-one destroyers and six submarines to help find the *Bismarck* and sink her. In the process each side had lost her mightiest warship.

It remained now only for the British to give the world the climactic news.

At eleven o'clock on the morning of May 27, 1941, Prime Minister Winston Churchill rose in the House of

Commons in London to make a report. The ancient seat of the British Parliament on the Thames had been bombed out. The Commons was meeting in nearby Church House.

> This morning [Churchill said], shortly after daylight, the *Bismarck*, virtually at a standstill, far from help, was attacked by the British pursuing battleships.
>
> I do not know what were the results of the bombardment. It appears, however, that the *Bismarck* was not sunk by gunfire. She will now be dispatched by torpedo . . .

He had barely sat down when a note was passed to him. He rose again.

> I ask the indulgence of the House. I have just received news that the *Bismarck* is sunk.

The House, Churchill commented later, "seemed content." The *Hood* had been avenged. The next day he cabled President Franklin D. Roosevelt in Washington, D.C.: "I will send you later the inside story of the fighting with the *Bismarck*. She was a terrific ship . . ."

At noon on May 27 German Naval Group West picked up from London a radio bulletin from Reuters, the British news-gathering agency. It announced the end of the *Bismarck*.

At 1:22 P.M., according to the German secret naval records, Group West sent out a coded radio message addressed to Admiral Luetjens:

REUTERS REPORTS BISMARCK SUNK. REPORT SITUATION IMMEDIATELY!

There was, of course, no response.

Never again in the four more years that World War II was to last did a German battleship venture out into the wide Atlantic.

AFTERWORD

THE SINKING OF THE *BISMARCK* WAS BUT THE OPENING chapter in the death of the battleship. Until 1941, it was thought that battleships were the ultimate seagoing weapons. Their guns could shoot with deadly accuracy for over twenty miles. Their hulls were heavily armored and it was thought that they were virtually unsinkable by torpedoes or by attack from the air.

In fact, it took almost fifty ships from the British Navy to locate and ultimately sink the *Bismarck*, the biggest and most deadly battleship ever built. However, it was a torpedo from a Swordfish, a small bi-plane, which ultimately crippled the *Bismarck* so that it became easy prey for the British fleet.

Six months later several other battleships were destroyed by small aircraft—the *Prince of Wales* (which was companion to the *Hood* in the Battle of Denmark Strait) and the *Repulse* were sunk by Japanese aircraft off Singapore on December 10, 1941, and, of course, three days earlier nine American battleships were either severely damaged or sunk by the Japanese surprise attack on Pearl Harbor.

The airplanes that made the Pearl Harbor attack were from Japanese aircraft carriers operating far from the Hawaiian Islands. The age of the battleship was over and the age of the carrier had just begun. In fact, the next two great sea battles of World War II were between opposing aircraft carrier forces—the Battle of the Coral Sea and the Battle of Midway. Sixty-five years after the *Bismarck* was sunk, aircraft carriers are still the most powerful seagoing weapons of navies around the world.

THE EDITORS

A NOTE ON SOURCES

All who write of the sinking of the *Bismarck* are indebted to Captain Russell Grenfell of the Royal Navy for his brilliant book, *The Bismarck Episode*. After the war he questioned all the British naval officers who took part in the chase, from Admirals of the Fleet, as they later became, Lord Tovey and Sir James Somerville on down. And he received much material from the Admiralty and other British official sources.

The official British account of the great drama at sea is given in Volume I of *The War at Sea* by Captain S. W. Roskill. This is part of the United Kingdom Military History Series.

I found much fascinating German material in the secret German Naval Archives, which were captured by the Allies at the end of World War II. A mimeographed volume entitled *Führer Conferences on Naval Affairs*, 1941, gives the text of the messages exchanged between Admiral Luetjens on the *Bismarck* and German Naval Headquarters. It also contains the official confidential German naval report on the episode drawn up a few weeks afterward by Admiral

Kurt Assmann. Finally there is in it the story told by one of the surviving seamen who was picked up by a German submarine.

The best German book I have seen on the subject is Fritz Otto Busch's *Das Geheimnis der Bismarck* (*The Secret of the Bismarck*). Busch was an officer on the cruiser *Prinz Eugen*. Admiral Friederich Ruge has also given a good account in his book, *Der Seekrieg, 1939–45* (*The War at Sea, 1939–45*).

Sir Winston Churchill gave a memorable picture of the drama as it looked to him from London in *The Grand Alliance*, the third volume of his memoirs of the Second World War.

W.L.S.

Index

ABOUT THE AUTHOR

WILLIAM SHIRER was one of the last century's greatest reporters and historians. After graduating from college in 1925, he headed across the Atlantic in a cattle boat and began working as a reporter for the *Chicago Tribune*, the *International Herald Tribune*, and the Universal News Service. He traveled extensively throughout Europe and Asia, reporting on such events as Lindbergh's solo flight across the Atlantic and the League of Nations meetings in Switzerland. Ultimately he joined CBS as a radio correspondent and began reporting on the rise of Adolph Hitler and Naziism from Berlin.

In late 1940 he was forced to flee from Germany. Luckily he was able to smuggle out his diaries and notes. He used them to write *Berlin Diary*, the best-selling story of his years in Germany. Later he wrote his most famous book, *The Rise and Fall of the Third Reich*, a detailed history of Hitler's Germany.

Mr. Shirer was one of the rare journalists who made the transition from reporter to historian.

BOOKS IN THIS SERIES

Abraham Lincoln: Friend of the People
BY CLARA INGRAM JUDSON

Admiral Richard Byrd: Alone in the Antarctic
BY PAUL RINK

Alexander the Great
BY JOHN GUNTHER

Amelia Earhart: Flying Solo
BY JOHN BURKE

The Barbary Pirates
BY C. S. FORESTER

Battle in the Arctic Seas
BY THEODORE TAYLOR

Behind Enemy Lines: A Young Pilot's Story
BY H. R. DEMALLIE

Ben Franklin: Inventing America
BY THOMAS FLEMING

Danger in the Desert: True Adventures of a Dinosaur Hunter
BY ROGER COHEN

Daniel Boone: The Opening of the Wilderness
BY JOHN MASON BROWN

General George Patton: Old Blood and Guts
BY ALDEN HATCH

George Washington: Frontier Colonel
BY STERLING NORTH

Geronimo: Wolf of the Warpath
BY RALPH MOODY

✳ STERLING POINT BOOKS